WALKING WITH
PAUL
Greece Travel Guide

ILLUSTRATION BY THÉODORE CARUELLE D'ALIGNY, 1846

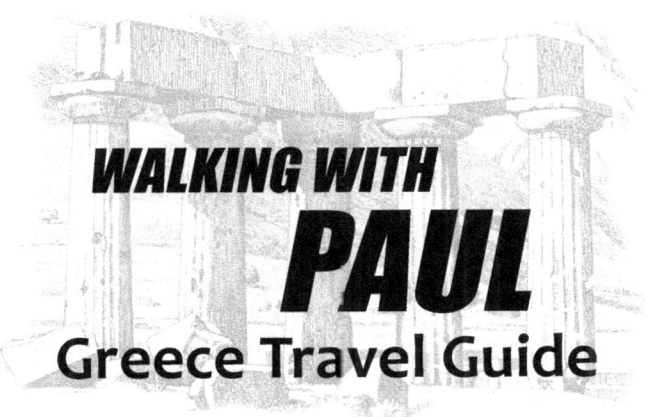

WALKING WITH
PAUL
Greece Travel Guide

Kenneth E. Mills

ILLUSTRATION BY THÉODORE CARUELLE D'ALIGNY, 1846

Walking With Paul
Greece Travel Guide

Published by Kenneth E. Mills
Searcy, Arkansas USA

Copyright © 2025 by Kenneth E. Mills

All rights reserved

ISBN 979-8-9994980-0-7

ISBN 979-8-9994980-1-4 (ebook)

Library of Congress Control Number: 2025916381

Dedication

This work is lovingly dedicated to my wonderful wife, Kay Mills, and our precious daughters, Rebecca and Jennifer. You have loved me, forgiven me, been patient with me, encouraged me, laughed and cried with me, and blessed me more than I deserve. I love you, and I will always love you. It is my prayer that we will always be faithful to our Lord and Savior Jesus Christ and honor Him every day in everything we do. We serve a risen Savior.

I am blessed.

To God be the glory.

Contents

Charts & Maps

Foreword

You have seen photographs of the Grand Canyon and the pyramids of Egypt. But have you seen them in person? For those who have done both, all would agree that photographs fail to do them justice. The reality of the visit far outstrips the photographs.

A visit to the lands of the Bible presents similarly dramatic contrasts. Nothing can substitute for standing and walking in (and smelling and sometimes feeling) the world of the events of the Bible. I have made literally dozens of trips throughout the eastern Mediterranean world and never fail to return without a deeper understanding and appreciation of the events and settings of God's interactions with us.

Some of these trips have been coordinated by and with Kenneth Mills and his wife Kay. In this volume, Kenneth has compiled a handy, brief orientation to numerous sites associated with the life and ministry of the apostle Paul. While this volume has value as a stand-alone production, he has designed it to be a ready-reference to places one would visit on a trek in Paul's wake.

The information provides quick access to basic historical and archaeological data relative to the various sites and regions. He does not burden us with exhaustive accounts for each site — instead he offers a kind of hors d'oeuvre to the main course of an actual visit. Of course, it will also serve as an excellent reminder for later reflection and review.

A valuable feature of Mills' work is the addition of spiritual reflections at various sites. Most who would travel Paul's itinerary are people of faith, and Mills offers suitable introspective comments and questions throughout the travel, prompting us to evaluate our relationship with our Savior in a more meaningful light.

It is an honor to commend Mills' work. He and Kay are gracious people whose care and love of the Lord is readily apparent. This book will be a blessing to have when you travel to Greece.

DALE W. MANOR, PH.D.
Professor Emeritus of Archaeology and Bible
    Harding University
Archaeological Field Director
    Tel Beth-Shemesh Excavations, Israel

Dr. Dale W. Manor positions a single-serving cooking juglet in a display case. The juglet dates from about 1000 BC.

With Grateful Appreciation

My parents, James and Jimmie Lee Mills, were people of faith. I saw their love for our Lord and Savior Jesus Christ and their love for each other. They encouraged me by their example and teaching to be faithful to God and His holy word.

Mother was my Sunday school teacher for a few years. When Daddy preached in Tomball, Texas, I remember going to the church building with him on Saturdays and hearing him preach to the pews in preparation for Sunday services. After we moved to Ennis, Texas, Daddy was my Sunday morning preacher for many years at Reagor Springs. I am eternally grateful for their leading me in God's holy will.

My sister Deanna also deserves credit as we were in Bible classes together over the years. And she normally found the chapter and verse first, got the correct answer before I did, and wound up with a higher score when testing!

My godly grandparents were a most wonderful blessing. During my elementary years in Ennis, Texas, we lived just a few blocks from Granddad and Mama Dee Layton. We were a little farther from Pop and Mom Mills who lived in Durant, Oklahoma. However, they all had this in common: their faithfulness to Jesus Christ, their love for each other, and their service to others.

Throughout my life, I've been blessed by my brothers and sisters in churches in which I've served and ministered.

For over 10 years, I preached on Sunday mornings for the Chastain Church of Christ in Arkansas. Though small in number, these people were generous in heart and pocketbook. In 1994, they sent me on my first tour of Israel.

When I made that first trip to Israel, Abed W. El Hawash was my guide. Abed was an excellent guide and helped open my eyes to the history, geography, and majesty of this marvelous country. It wasn't too long before I returned to Israel.

When I first met Dr. Dale W. Manor and heard him teach, I knew that I was going to be blessed. As one who served in local ministry for 25 years and who has served in the academic world for over 25 years at Harding University, Dr. Manor has encouraged and challenged me in my knowledge of the scriptures and understanding of their settings.

As Dr. Manor and I have traveled together and led tours in Israel, Egypt, Türkiye, and Greece, we've worked with excellent travel partners and had superb guides in planning and operating tours.

I've been blessed to stand on Mars Hill in Athens and catch a glimpse of what Paul saw as he preached to people who did not know Jesus. I've walked along the Via Egnatia in Philippi. I've touched the waters of the Sea of Galilee where Jesus walked and taught. I've sailed on the Nile and viewed the Great Pyramid of Giza. I've marveled at the Great Theatre in Ephesus where people cried out, "Great is Artemis of the Ephesians!"

To the many who have traveled with me: "Thank you!" It is rewarding to travel and see these wonderful historic sites. It is more rewarding to see the response of people as they remember Peter's confession at Caesarea Philippi, have a devotional at Lydia's baptismal site, walk the streets of Corinth, or pause at the tomb of Jesus. To see it in their eyes… to hear it in their voice… Lives are being changed as they develop a deeper understanding and greater appreciation of God's holy word.

Preface

When I sat down to write this book, my brain was somewhat like scrambled eggs because so many thoughts were going through my mind on how to approach this project. My ultimate goal was to create a book which would give people thumbnail sketches of sites they would see in Greece that relate to Paul's second missionary journey. At the same time, I'm including other locations of historical and cultural interest that are not too far off the path of Paul's journey.

Although we're focusing on Greece, we begin our tour in Istanbul, Türkiye. This allows us to enter Greece and follow Paul's journey in a chronological order as we did on a recent tour. We later return to Türkiye and conclude our travels at Ephesus and Miletus.

On many of these cities, I give limited background information. This is not intended to be a thorough history of the city, but rather it gives a glimpse of events that helped form the area.

Dates are sometimes difficult, and excellent scholars will come to different conclusions. The Gallio Inscription which is in the Archaeological Museum of Delphi gives a time frame on when Gallio was proconsul of Achaia. Because Paul stood before him in Corinth (Acts 18:23 ff), this gives us the dates Paul was in Corinth. Some scholars date 51 as the time Gallio was in Achaia; others 52.

As a rule, I use BC for dates before the birth of Christ but do not use AD for dates after Christ unless I feel it is needed for clarification.

Sometimes there are differences on what took place where. Socrates died in Athens. Did he die in the Prison of Socrates or in the Athens State Prison? Sources differ.

All photos/illustrations are my work unless otherwise noted.

"I wish I had…" is probably a statement that I will make many times after the book is published because there are always things you wish you had included or phrased differently or on which you had given additional information. Even after the book is published, it will continue to be a living project in my life for a long time to come.

Most of all, I want this to be a tool which will help you as you travel to sites where Paul lived, taught, and served. As you look at his life, may you be encouraged to walk closer to God and serve Him more faithfully.

Introduction

Confronted... Convicted... Consumed...

As one stands on Mars Hill when visiting Athens, Greece, there is a sense of awe mixed with wonderment: awe because of standing where the apostle Paul preached the gospel of Jesus Christ almost 2,000 years ago; wonderment because of wanting to know more about what he was thinking as he stood on this plain nondescript rock surrounded by majestic marble temples.

In this guide book, we'll be taking a journey with the apostle Paul following in his footsteps as he preached the gospel of Jesus Christ in Asia Minor and Europe. This will be in the form of a travelogue as one might tour the area today with our main focus being with the time he spent in Macedonia and Achaia — what is now Greece — on his second missionary journey (Acts 15:36–18:22).

The foundation for Paul's missionary journeys into Asia Minor, Macedonia, and Achaia began long before his actual arrival to those areas of the world. One might say it was when he was on his way to persecute Christians in Damascus and a light brighter than the sun shown around him.

Perhaps Paul, as a zealous Jew who was opposing the name of Jesus, had made other journeys before, but this journey to Damascus was a life-changing event. As he related this experience after being arrested in the temple, he stated, "As I was on my way and drew near to Damascus, about noon a great light from heaven suddenly shown around me. And I fell to the ground and heard a voice saying to me, 'Saul, Saul, why are you persecuting me?'" (Acts 22:6-7).

Paul revealed that it was Jesus speaking to him, and he was told to go into Damascus to learn what he was to do. He could not see because he had been blinded by the brightness of the light, so those with him led him.

While in Damascus, Ananias came to see him and restored his sight. Ananias then said, "The God of our fathers appointed you to know his will, to see the Righteous One and to hear a voice from his mouth... And now why do you wait? Rise and be baptized and wash away your sins, calling on his name" (Acts 22:14, 16).

This took place just a few years after the death, burial, resurrection, and ascension of Christ Jesus into heaven.

Paul's zealousness moved from one persecuting Christians to one passionately proclaiming the gospel of Jesus Christ. Yet, because of his former life, many people did not believe him. When he tried to join with the Christians in Jerusalem, they were afraid of him (Acts 9:26). After all, he held the coats of those who stoned Stephen (Acts 7:58) and had developed a reputation as one who was destroying the church of Jesus Christ (Acts 8:3).

Barnabas, whose name means "son of encouragement," became Paul's encourager, mentor, and fellow evangelist.

Paul later wrote to the Christians at Galatia about what took place between the time he became a Christian and when he began his evangelistic missions. He was apparently gone from Jerusalem for about three years while being in Arabia most of that time.

We don't have any indication that Paul was involved in evangelistic work when he was in Arabia. Rather, it seems to be a time when Paul learned about the fullness of the gospel — not from man — but from Jesus Christ (Galatians 1:11-12). He stated that God "was pleased to reveal his Son to me, in order that I might preach him among the Gentiles" (Galatians 1:16). At the beginning of this letter, he gave his credentials as being an apostle sent by Jesus Christ and God the Father (Galatians 1:1).

Several years after he returned to Jerusalem and had gone up to Antioch, the Holy Spirit called for Paul and Barnabas to be set apart "for the work to which I have called them" (Acts 13:2).

This first missionary journey took them to Cyprus and the regions of Pamphylia and Galatia in what is now modern-day Türkiye (formerly known as the Republic of Turkey). This journey possibly took 12-18 months.

When Paul had gone to Jerusalem after becoming a Christian, he faced rejection because these people knew who he was and how he had persecuted the church. On this first journey, Paul faced resistance; he faced the departure of a coworker; he was insulted; he was stoned and left for dead. But Paul was called to preach the gospel of Jesus Christ, and that is what he did throughout his life — even to the point of death.

As we travel with Paul on his journeys, may we see his completely undivided commitment to living for and proclaiming the message of Jesus. In doing so, may we remember what he wrote the Christians at Corinth, "Be imitators of me, as I am of Christ" (1 Corinthians 11:1).

May we also remember the example of Barnabas — and as God's people be people who encourage, set godly examples, and mentor others in the holy will of God.

"Therefore encourage one another and build one another up, just as you are doing" (1 Thessalonians 5:11).

Let's begin our journey with Paul.

— PAUL'S 2ND MISSIONARY JOURNEY —
FROM THE MACEDONIAN CALL TO HIS DEPARTURE FROM EPHESUS

Chapter 1

Beginning the Journey

After a period of time had passed since their first missionary journey, Paul and Barnabas had a desire to return and see how these new churches were doing.

But there was a problem. Barnabas' cousin, John Mark, had started the first journey but had returned home after a little while. Barnabas wanted to take John Mark on the second journey, but Paul didn't. Both sides had their points: Barnabas is the one who encouraged people who had been rejected. Paul wanted a dependable coworker. This resulted in two missionary journeys: Barnabas took John Mark; Paul took Silas and was later joined by Timothy and Luke.

> Barnabas' characteristic of encouraging people was a trait that Paul learned. As he was nearing the end of his life, he wrote Timothy saying, "Get Mark [Barnabas' cousin] and bring him with you, for he is very useful to me for ministry." (2 Timothy 4:11).

Prior to this second journey, the issue of circumcision had arisen (Acts 15). The apostles and elders met in Jerusalem and made a decision on this issue. They sent a letter with Paul, Barnabas, Judas, and Silas to Antioch (vv. 23-29). As they traveled from town to town on this second journey, Paul and Silas delivered "the decisions that had been reached by the apostles and elders who were in Jerusalem" (Acts 16:4).

After Paul and Silas left Antioch, they went through Syria and Cilicia strengthening the churches. They then arrived in Derbe and Lystra, two cities that Barnabas and Paul had visited on their earlier journey.

Timothy was a disciple who lived at Lystra. We don't know if this is Paul's first encounter with him or if they had met on the first journey. Timothy's mother was a believing Jew, and his father was a Greek.

The Bible tells us, "He was well spoken of by the brothers at Lystra and Iconium." (Acts 16:2). Paul took Timothy with them and thus became a mentor to him.

They traveled through Phrygia and Galatia and wanted to enter Bithynia, "but the Spirit of Jesus did not allow them" (Acts 16:7). They went to Troas. It was here that Paul had a vision of a man from Macedonia begging him to "Come over to Macedonia and help us" (Acts 16:9). Paul concluded that God had called them to preach the Gospel to that region.

Entering the Topkopi Palace Museum through the Middle Gate, also known as the "Gate of Salutation."

Chapter 2

Istanbul – A City on Two Continents

41.0063202, 28.9757677 / 41° 0′ 22.753″ N 28° 58′ 32.764″ E

As we begin our journey to follow Paul's footsteps in Greece on his second missionary journey, we fly into Istanbul, Türkiye (formerly the Republic of Turkey — now the Republic of Türkiye).

This allows us to see a little of the culture of what was Asia Minor and also gives us the opportunity to follow Paul's journey in chronological order when we arrive in Greece.

Istanbul is a city which sits on two continents: Europe and Asia. The Bosphorus Strait runs through the city and connects the Black Sea to the Sea of Marmara. It is a city of about 16 million people. About 65% of the population lives on the European side of the Bosphorus.

> We don't have any record of the apostle Paul being in the city we know as Istanbul (ancient Byzantium). Had the Holy Spirit allowed Paul to go to Bithynia, would Paul have made his way westward to Byzantium and then into Macedonia at a later point?

History of the City —

The area of Istanbul has a long and storied history. It was originally a port settlement called Lygos according to Pliny the Elder. This would have been between the 13th and 11th centuries BC. In recent years, archaeologists have uncovered artifacts that date back as far as the 6th millennium BC.

About 657 BC, the city was founded by Greek settlers from Megara and given the name Byzantium. In 513 BC, the city was taken by Darius the Great of the Persian Empire.

After the Battle of Plataea in 479 BC, the Spartans took control from the Persians. In 408 BC, the city was captured by Athens. In 340 BC,

Philip II of Macedon was unsuccessful in his attempt to gain control of the city.

In 196, Roman Emperor Septimius Severus captured the city.

In 312, Constantine the Great began to embrace Christianity. After defeating Maxentius at the Battle of the Melvian Bridge, he became the sole ruler of the Western Roman Empire.

Constantine made Byzantium the capital of the Roman Empire in 330 and gave it a new name, Constantinople, naming it after himself.

Intervening years saw Roman leadership changes and many developments in the city. Among these was a brief control by the Latin Empire from 1204-1261. In 1261, Byzantines regained control of Constantinople.

On May 29, 1453, Mehmed II conquered Constantinople marking the end of the Byzantine Empire and transforming the city into the capital of the Ottoman Empire.

After the Turkish War of Independence (May 19, 1919 – July 24, 1923) and the establishment of the Republic of Turkey (October 29, 1923), Ankara became the capital. Constantinople was renamed Istanbul in 1930. Mustafa Kemal became its first president.

Our nation has succeeded owing to the unshakable unity it has shown in its actions and endeavors. — *Mustafa Kemal Atatürk*

Prior to becoming president of Turkey, Mustafa Kemal was a respected military leader. He championed many social, cultural, and economic reforms. In 1934, the national assembly gave him the surname of Atatürk which means "Father of the Turks." Mustafa Kemal Atatürk served as president until November 10, 1938. He is highly revered.

Sites To See —

In visiting Istanbul, the Fatih district is home to many historical and religious sites. The Fatih District is on the European side of Istanbul where the Bosphorus Strait connects with the Sea of Marmara.

Sultanahmet Square —

41.0063202, 28.9757677 / 41° 0′ 22.753″ N 28° 58′ 32.764″ E

Sultanahmet Square in Istanbul was originally a hippodrome constructed in 203 by Emperor Septimius Severus. When Emperor Constantine rebuilt the city in 324, he expanded the Hippodrome and renamed it — what else? — the Hippodrome of Constantinople. It was estimated to be 1,476 feet long and 427 feet wide. Its stands could hold a crowd of 100,000.

The square, which is actually a rectangle running from southwest to northeast, offers a lively environment and contains ancient and historical structures. They include:

Walled Obelisk —

41.0053534, 28.9748572 / 1° 0′ 19.272″ N   28° 58′ 29.486″ E

This 105 foot-high obelisk is constructed of rough cut stones. The origination of the obelisk is unknown, but it does date back to the Middle Ages. At one time it was faced with bronze plates, but in 1204 they were removed by crusaders and melted down.

Serpent Column —

41.0056044, 28.9751336 / 41° 0′ 20.176″ N   28° 58′ 30.481″ E

Consisting of three intertwined snakes, this column was originally located in Delphi. It celebrated the Greek victory over the Persian Empire at the Battle of Plataea in 479 BC. Constantine moved the column to grace the Hippodrome of Constantinople. There is a reproduction of it at Delphi.

Obelisk of Theodosius —

41.0058655, 28.9754099 / 41° 0′ 21. 16″ N   28° 58′ 31.476″ E

This obelisk was erected in Karnak, Egypt, during the reign of Pharaoh Thutmose III (1479-1425 BC). Roman emperor Constantius II transported it and another obelisk to Alexandria, Egypt. In 390, Roman Emperor Theodosius, who ruled from 379 to 395, had it transported to Constantinople.

German Fountain —

41.0070530, 28.9767109 / 41° 0′ 25.391″ N   28° 58′ 36.159″ E

This beautiful fountain was constructed in 1900 to commemorate German Emperor Wilhelm II's visit to Istanbul in 1898.

As one travels from the southeast side of Sultanahmet Square toward the northeast, there are a number of sites of interest.

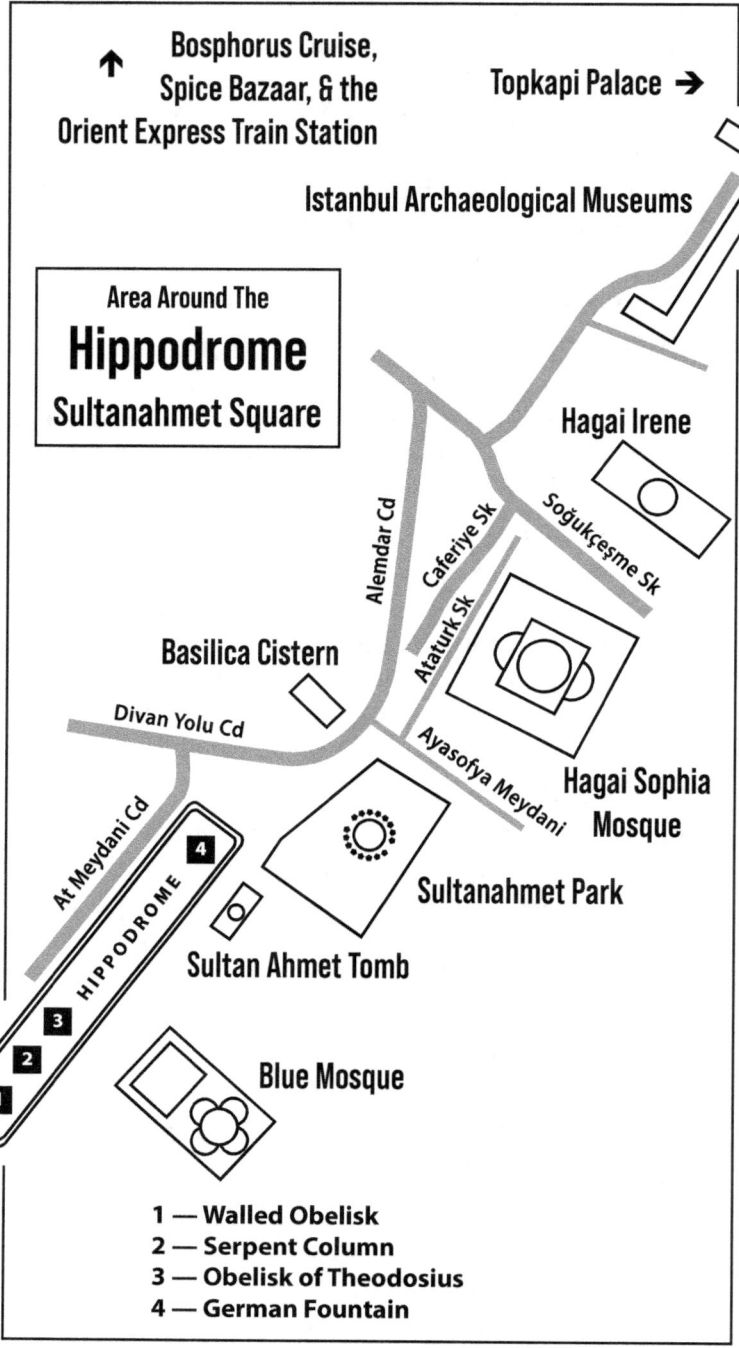

Bosphorus Cruise, Spice Bazaar, & the Orient Express Train Station ↑

Topkapi Palace →

Istanbul Archaeological Museums

Area Around The
Hippodrome
Sultanahmet Square

Hagai Irene

Alemdar Cd

Caferiye Sk

Soğukçeşme Sk

Ataturk Sk

Basilica Cistern

Divan Yolu Cd

Ayasofya Meydani

Hagai Sophia Mosque

Sultanahmet Park

At Meydani Cd

HIPPODROME

4

Sultan Ahmet Tomb

3

2

1

Blue Mosque

1 — Walled Obelisk
2 — Serpent Column
3 — Obelisk of Theodosius
4 — German Fountain

Blue Mosque —

41.0054541, 28.9767066 / 41° 0′ 19.635″ N 28° 58′ 36.144″ E

Between 1609 and 1617, the Blue Mosque was constructed during the rule of Ahmed I. Its official name is Sultan Ahmed Mosque. The design is classical Ottoman with a large central dome surrounded by four smaller semi-domes. The mosque has six minarets. Because of the blue tiles used to decorate the interior, it became known as the Blue Mosque.

Sultanahmet Park —

41.0071848, 28.9782745 / 41° 0′ 25.865″ N 28° 58′ 41.788″ E

Located between the Blue Mosque and Hagia Sophia is the Sultanahmet Park. It has exquisite landscaping, beautiful flowers, and a relaxing fountain.

The Hagia Sophia Grand Mosque was originally constructed by Byzantine emperor Justinian I as a Christian cathedral in Constantinople. It was completed in 537 and has served as a Christian church, Orthodox church, mosque, and museum. On July 10, 2020, the Council of State decreed that the site could only serve as a mosque.

Hagia Sophia Grand Mosque —
41.0084924, 28.9798134 / 41° 0' 30.573" N   28° 58' 47.328" E

In 537, Justinian I completed and dedicated the Hagia Sophia — the Church of Divine Wisdom. It is an engineering masterpiece because it has a 108-foot diameter dome resting on four triangular segments over a square room. After conquering Constantinople, Sultan Mehmet II converted it to a mosque. The four minarets were then added. In 1935, Atatürk made it a museum. On Friday, July 10, 2020, the Council of Ministers revoked the museum status allowing President Tayyip Erdoğan to declare Hagia Sophia a mosque.

Basilica Cistern —
41.0083569, 28.9779257 / 41° 0' 30.085" N   28° 58' 40.533" E

Located about 500 feet west of the Hagia Sophia, the Basilica Cistern dates back to the 6th century having been built during the reign of Emperor Justinian I. It contains 330 marble and granite columns. The cistern was one of the locations used in the 1963 James Bond film, *From Russia with Love.*

Hagia Irene —
41.0096138, 28.9810784 / 41° 0' 34.610" N   28° 58' 51.882" E

Constantine the Great commissioned the building of the Hagia Irene in 330, and it was completed in 337, the year he died. It is an Eastern Orthodox Church and is the oldest known church in Istanbul. It sits in the outer courtyard of Topkapi Palace.

Topkapi Palace —
41.0113030, 28.9831470 / 41° 0' 40.691" N   28° 58' 59.329" E

After conquering Constantinople May 29, 1453, Sultan Mehmed II built the magnificent Topkapi Palace. With construction beginning in 1460 and being completed in 1478, Topkapi Palace is an architectural masterpiece. It contains four courtyards, a harem, library, and a jewel-filled treasury, among other sections. It opened as a museum in 1924 and allows one to see history, culture, and marvelous collections from the Ottoman Empire.

Istanbul Archaeological Museums —
41.0116043, 28.9814006 / 41° 0' 41.775" N   28° 58' 53.042" E

Neighboring the area of Topkapi Palace are the Istanbul Archaeological Museums. The Archaeology Museum, The Museum of the Ancient Orient, and The Tiled Kiosk Museum are the three major sections of the museum. It was founded in 1985 by Osman Hamdi Bey because so many of the region's ancient artifacts were being shipped to European museums. The museums contain treasures from Assyrian, Hittite, Egyptian, Greek, Roman, Byzantine, Canaanite, Israelite, and Ottoman civilizations.

Bosphorus Strait —

41.0573501, 29.0456067 /
41° 3′ 26.460″ N   29° 2′ 44.184″ E

The Bosphorus Strait connects the Black Sea to the north with the Sea of Marmara to the south. From the Sea of Marmara you can transition to the beautiful blue Aegean Sea. The strait also separates European Istanbul from Asian Istanbul. Various cruises, including dinner cruises, are available on the Bosphorus.

ABOVE — *The chapel at Hagia Irene has tremendous acoustics and is a great place to sing praises to our God.*

LEFT — *The city of Istanbul is known for its tulips, and there were many beautiful blooms in the courtyard of Topkapi Palace.*

BELOW — *The nighttime lights of Istanbul reflect in the Golden Horn which connects with the Bosphorus Strait in Istanbul.* — PHOTO BY DAVID KNIGHT

Rumeli Fortress —

41.0847575, 29.0567648 / 41° 5′ 5.127″ N   29° 3′ 24.353″ E

In 1452, this fortress was built by Ottoman Sultan Mehmed II on the narrowest point of the Bosphorus Strait. It was located at that point to prohibit aid from the north from reaching the Byzantine Empire. It later became a prison. The towers are some of the largest in the world. Today, it serves as a museum, and you can enjoy a spectacular view of the Bosphorus from its garden, or you will have a great view of the fortress when you take a Bosphorus cruise.

Dolmabahçe Palace —

41.0388807, 29.0006346 / 41° 2′ 19.971″ N   29° 0′ 2.285″ E

With 285 rooms, Dolmabahçe Palace is the largest palace in Türkiye. Its construction was ordered by Sultan Abdulmejid I and built between the years 1843 and 1856. It was home to six Sultans until the abolition of the Caliphate in 1924. If you choose not to take a tour of it, you can still have a great view of it as you cruise the Bosphorus.

Spice Bazaar —

41.0164265, 28.9706393 / 41° 0′ 59.135″ N   28° 58′ 14.301″ E

Built in 1664, this bazaar is known in Turkish as Mısır Çarşısı. It is also referred to as the Egyptian Bazaar because of being built with Ottoman funds from Egypt. This colorful bazaar consists of about 80 shops selling spices, sweets, dates, dried fruit, nuts, jewelry, and souvenirs. It is an excellent place to visit right after a Bosphorus cruise because of its proximity to the cruise dock.

Grand Bazaar —

41.0106601, 28.9683641 / 41° 0′ 38.376″ N   28° 58′ 6.111″ E

This is the world's oldest and largest shopping center having almost 4,000 shops. Construction began in 1455 during the reign of Sultan Mehmed II. You can spend days in the Grand Bazaar, find just about anything, and kindly negotiate your price.

Yedikule Fortress —

40.9932140, 28.9232084 / 40° 59′ 35.570″ N   28° 55′ 23.550″ E

This "Fortress of Seven Towers" was commissioned by Ottoman Sultan Mehmed II and completed in 1458. It included the Golden Gate which Theodosius built during the Byzantine period as the main ceremonial gate to the city. The gate is the eastern end of the Via Egnatia.

In addition to being a defensive structure, the fortress also served as a prison.

Chora Church —
41.0311798, 28.9391623 / 41° 1′ 52.247″ N 28° 56′ 20.984″ E

Dating back to the 4th century, the Chora Church was part of a monastery. It is famous because of its example of Byzantine architecture, mosaics, and frescoes. In the 16th century it was converted into a mosque. In 1945, the Turkish government turned it into a museum.

Gracing the gardens outside the Yedikule Fortress in Istanbul is a spirited silver steed. — PHOTO BY KAY MILLS

Ecumenical Patriarchate of Constantinople —
41.0291262, 28.9518748 / 41° 1′ 44.854″ N 28° 57′ 6.749″ E

Also encompassing the 18th century Church of St George, the Patriarchate serves as the spiritual center of the Orthodox Church.

The Church of the Holy Apostles —
41.0195674, 28.9500094 / 41° 1′ 10.443″ N 28° 57′ 0.034″ E

When Constantine died in 337, he was originally buried at The Church of The Holy Apostles which had been dedicated in 330. In 397, John Chrysostom was appointed Archbishop of Constantinople. The church later held the relics of Chrysostom and others. In 550, the church was rebuilt. The church remained until 1461. In 1470, the construction of the Fatih Mosque was completed on the site.

Fatih Mosque —
41.0195674, 28.9500094 / 41° 1′ 10.443″ N 28° 57′ 0.034″ E

The Fatih Mosque was constructed between 1463 and 1470. After an earthquake in 1766, it was reconstructed with a different design. The mosque once housed the Sahn-ı Seman Medrese which was founded by astronomer Ali Qushji. It focused on the study of theology, law, medicine, astronomy, physics, and mathematics. The mosque has been restored a couple of times in recent years. It sits on the site where The Church of the Holy Apostles was once located.

Religion in Istanbul —

Religious Affiliation: About 90% of Istanbul residents identify as Sunni Muslims. Some reports state that 99% of the population identifies as Muslim. Religious minorities include Greek Orthodox Christians, Armenian Christians, Catholic Levantines, Assyrian Christians, and Sephardic Jews. In 2000, it was reported there were 2,691 active mosques, 123 active churches, and 20 active synagogues in Istanbul.

Reflections …

As we tour this city with over 2,600 mosques, we remember that at one point in history it was what some would describe as a Christian city. What caused the change? How rooted are we in our faith in Jesus Christ? How moved are we when we hear the call of Jesus Christ?

Chapter 3

Evangelism in Western Türkiye

As we study God's word, there are times we read about a church, but we don't have record of its origin. This is the case of the some of the seven churches of The Revelation to John from Jesus Christ — churches which were in Asia Minor now modern-day Türkiye.

The seven churches were Ephesus, Smyrna, Pergamum, Thyatira, Sardis, Philadelphia, and Laodicea. We learn about the establishment of the church in Ephesus on Paul's second and third missionary journeys. The only other mention of Thyatira is in Acts 16:14 where it was listed as Lydia's hometown.

Christians at Laodicea are mentioned in Paul's letter to the church at Colossae. In the same letter, Paul also references the church in Hierapolis.

However, Smyrna, Pergamum, Sardis, and Philadelphia are mentioned only in The Revelation.

So… from where did these churches come? There are several possibilities including:

On the day of Pentecost many nations were present. Included in that group were people from Cappadocia, Pontus, Asia, Phrygia, and Pamphylia. These regions make up modern-day Türkiye. Many who responded to the gospel and were baptized into Jesus Christ were probably from these areas.

In his letter to the Christians at Colossae, Paul referred to their hearing the gospel of Jesus Christ from Epaphras (Colossians 1: 6-8).

When Paul began his third missionary journey (Acts 18:23-21:26), he traveled through Galatia and Phrygia "strengthening all the disciples" (Acts 18:23). Later, he expressed his interest in visiting Rome but "he himself stayed in Asia for a while" (Acts 19:22).

Paul made a brief visit to Ephesus on his second journey, but stayed there for about three years on his third journey. With travel in the region, one would think that people from other cities, towns, and villages might come to Ephesus at times. Luke stated that Paul held daily discussions in the hall of Tyrannus for two years (Acts 19:9-10). Also, it is easy to think about Paul taking a few days every several weeks to travel throughout the region — much like an old-time circuit-riding evangelist.

Expansion of the church may harken back to the time when Paul was persecuting the church, and believers in Jerusalem were "scattered throughout the regions of Judea and Samaria" (Acts 8:1). Over the next few years, this scattering reached people from other parts of the world "as far as Phoenicia and Cyprus and Antioch" (Acts 11:19).

However the church spread, may we remember Paul's message to the Christians at Corinth: "I planted, Apollos watered, but God gave the growth." (1 Corinthians 3:6). Many may be involved in teaching and evangelism, but God is the One who brings growth — He is the One who gives life.

Chapter 4

Samothrace – A Stop in the Night

40.4531084, 25.5798204 / 40° 27′ 11.190″N 25° 34′ 47.353″E

When Paul was in Troas before coming to Macedonia, he had a vision of a man pleading, "Come over to Macedonia and help us" (Acts 16:9). Luke went on to say, "So, setting sail from Troas, we made a direct voyage to Samothrace, and the following day to Neapolis" (Acts 16:11).

Samothrace is an island in the northern Aegean Sea about 20 miles southwest of Alexandroupolis. It is 69 square miles and has a population of 2,596 spread among 15 communities.

It served as an anchor point for ships so sailors could rest during the night and not be on dangerous seas in the darkness. This appears to be what Paul and his companions did before continuing to Neapolis (Kavala, Greece). Whether he actually set foot on the island is not known.

It is a rugged island with a lot of granite and basalt, and Mount Fengari rises to a height of 5,285 feet. Because of its height, Mount Fengari was used by sailors for navigation. Homer stated that Poseidon, Greek god of the sea, storms, earthquakes, and horses, watched the Trojan War from the mountain peak.

From a historical/archaeological perspective, two discoveries stand out: the Sanctuary of the Great Gods and the Nike of Samothrace.

The Sanctuary of the Great Gods was built about 1000 BC by Thracians. It was the center for various activities including sacrifices, offerings, and worship to any of a number of gods. According to Plutarch, the future Macedonian king, Philip II, met Olympias at the site when they were still youth. They fell in love and later got married.

In 1863, Charles Champoiseau discovered the Nike of Samothrace as he was exploring the ruins of the Sanctuary of the Great Gods. Its total height is 18 feet, 3 inches and is now located in the Louvre in Paris.

Access to Samothrace is by ferry from the Port of Alexandroupolis. When one visits Samothrace, you will find great beaches along with nature and wildlife areas. Fishing and tourism are the main industries on Samothrace.

Chapter 5

Alexandroupolis – Maybe a Brief Visit

40.8461918, 25.8768820 / 40° 50′ 46.290″ N 25° 52′ 36.775″ E

After touring Istanbul for a couple of days, we cross the border and head to Kavala, Greece (ancient Neapolis). Shortly after crossing the border, we come to Alexandroupolis, Greece.

Alexandroupolis is a city of over 70,000 and serves as a crossroads of sea and land routes in eastern Greece. It was first settled as a fishing village in the 19th century and was known as Dedeağaç. In 1920, King Alexander I visited the city. The city fathers renamed the city Alexandroupolis, the city of Alexander.

The Lighthouse of Alexandroupolis is a symbol of the city. It began operating in 1880 and stands 88 feet above the sea level. Its light is visible for about 27 miles. It was initially illuminated with acetylene gas before being converted to oil. In 1974 it was changed over to electricity.

In the area you can visit Evros Delta National Park, Ethnological Museum of Thrace, the Thermal Springs of Traianoupoli, or Mesimbria-Zone, an archaeological site a few miles from Alexandroupolis. You may find time to tour Kyklopas Olive Mill, see the olive groves, and taste various olive products.

Chapter 6

Neapolis – The Modern Port of Kavala

40.9351232, 24.4082883 / 40° 56′ 6.444″ N   24° 24′ 29.838″ E

Founded in the late 7th century BC, Neapolis was one of several colonies on the coastline established by settlers from Thasos. The area was appealing because of gold and silver mines in the region. By the end of the 6th century BC, Neapolis declared its independence.

During the Peloponnesian War, Neapolis remained loyal to Athens. Philip II of Macedon later conquered Neapolis.

Along with having a harbor, the Via Egnatia passed through Neapolis. Both of these helped the city flourish economically.

Pictured above is the modern port of Kavala. Just as it was in the days when Paul sailed here, the port remains important to the commercial trade of the area.

It was here where Paul landed after hearing the Macedonian call (Acts 16:11).

On Paul's third missionary journey, he left Ephesus for Macedonia (Acts 20:1). The probability is that he went by sea to Neapolis. When he was returning to Troas, he sailed from Philippi (Acts 20:6). Neapolis would be the port city for Philippi.

From its establishment in the 7th century BC until the 9th century AD, the city was known as Neapolis. From the 9th century AD until the 14th century AD, it was known as Christoupolis — the city of Christ. It gained its current name, Kavala, in the 14th century AD.

The origin of the name Kavala may be a derivative of cavallo, which means horse in Italian. Because Kavala is on the Via Egnatia, it is reported to have been a stop where couriers changed horses.

When you stop in Kavala today, some impressive sites include:

The Kavala Fortress —
40.9344504, 24.4153433 / 40° 56′ 4.021″ N   24° 24′ 55.236″ E

Dating from the early 15th century, the fortress sits as a sentinel in the night.

Standing out against the city skyline is the ancient aqueduct. The aqueduct was in use until 1911.

The Kavala Aqueduct —
40.9369284, 24.4155054 / 40° 56′ 12.942″ N   24° 24′ 55.819″ E

This aqueduct was constructed in the 1500s at the height of the Ottoman Empire. It consists of 60 arches with the maximum height being about 82 feet tall and spanning a distance of 820 feet.

The Via Egnatia —
40.9403611, 24.3815619 / 40° 56′ 25.300″ N   24° 22′ 53.623″ E

The Via Egnatia runs through Kavala, and there are several places you can see it. You can also walk on it for a little distance. We cover its history in the next chapter.

Port of Kavala —

40.9346662, 24.4120603 / 40° 56′ 4.798″ N   24° 24′ 43.417″ E

It was somewhere in this area that the apostle Paul landed when he sailed over from Troas. There are several restaurants in the area where you can enjoy an excellent meal while viewing the activities in the harbor.

Eating in one of the restaurants alongside the harbor offers a great meal, cool breeze, and a magnificent view. My dog face shark was excellent!

USED BY PERMISSION OF ARTIST, ERIC GABA
WIKIMEDIA COMMONS USER: STING

Chapter 7

Via Egnatia – An Ancient Interstate

In the 2nd century BC, the Romans constructed the Via Egnatia. It was built to connect Roman colonies from Dyrrachium on the Adriatic Sea (modern day Durrës, Albania) to Byzantium (modern-day Istanbul, Türkiye) on the Bosphorous Strait. The terminal on the Adriatic Sea was across the sea from the Via Appia which led to Rome.

The road — almost 700 miles long — was named after Gnaeus Egnatius, proconsul of Macedonia, who ordered its construction. It was to be a road for soldiers, trade, and general travel.

When Paul arrived at Neapolis, he most certainly would have traveled the Via Egnatia from there to Philippi and on to Thessalonica before heading to Berea.

In Kavala (above), there is a 1,000 meter section of the Via Egnatia where one can walk along this ancient road.

In Philippi (left), a different type of stone was used, and you can see chariot ruts in many of the stones.

In Istanbul you can see the Golden Gate at Yedikule Fortress, the eastern terminus of the Via Egnatia. You can view sections of the Via Egnatia today in Alexandroupolis, Neapolis, and ancient Philippi, along with many other locations.

Adjacent to the Golden Gate of the Yedikule Fortress in Istanbul is the Small Golden Gate. — PHOTO BY KAY MILLS

Chapter 8

Philippi – The First European Convert

41.0112890, 24.2879612 / 41° 0′ 40.640″ N   24° 17′ 16.660″ E

In about 359 BC, colonists from the island of Thasos in the North Aegean Sea established what came to be known as Philippi. It was originally named Thasos, but after Philip II of Macedon conquered it in 356 BC, he named it after himself.

The city had much to be desired — partly because of gold mines in the area but also because of its proximity to the harbor at Neapolis (Kavala). The area came under Roman control after the Battle of Pydna in 168 BC.

After Macedon became a Roman province in 146 BC, the Romans built the Via Egnatia. That construction was a great benefit to Philippi. The Via Egnatia was connected to city center by a commercial street and solidified Philippi's position as a vital link in trade and communication.

In 42 BC, the Battle of Philippi took place. Mark Antony and Octavian defeated Brutus and Cassius, who had murdered Julius Caesar. Following this, Philippi became a Roman colony, and Octavian later became the Roman Emperor Augustus Caesar. He was ruler of the Roman Empire when both John the Baptist and Jesus Christ were born. He ordered the census Luke referenced in Luke 2:1.

During the time Paul was there, the city was prosperous.

By the 7th century, people abandoned the city because of large earthquakes and raids by the Slavics.

Paul in Philippi —

Much of Paul's mission approach was going to major cities and speaking to people at the local synagogue.

Philippi is defined as a "leading city of the district of Macedonia and a Roman colony" (Acts 16:12). However, it did not have a synagogue. But that did not keep believers from gathering on the Sabbath.

Luke wrote, "And on the Sabbath day we went outside the gate to the riverside, where we supposed there was a place of prayer" (Acts 16:13).

A couple of questions come up: 1) Why didn't Philippi have a synagogue, and 2) why did they expect to find a place of prayer?

Historically, you must have 10 adult Jewish males in order to have a synagogue. If you did not have that number, people could still meet and worship. That is probably what was happening in Philippi. Paul and those with him presumably heard about this from talk on the street or by asking around.

Ruins of buildings, columns, walls, monuments, and statues are scattered throughout Philippi.

Their work was not without results. One response came because of an open heart. The other response came because a soldier witnessed a Christ-like character.

When they went to the place of prayer at the river, they spoke to the women who had gathered there. One person was Lydia from Thyatira "who was a worshiper of God. The Lord opened her heart to pay attention to what was said by Paul" (Acts 16:14). The result was that she and members of her household were baptized into Jesus Christ. Lydia is the first known convert on European soil.

Another time they were going to the place of prayer and were met by a fortune-telling slave girl. Paul later commanded the spirit to come out of her in the name of Jesus. This — and their teachings — created an uproar. Paul and Silas were beaten and thrown into prison.

About midnight they were praying and singing. Prisoners were listening to them. An earthquake shook the doors open. The jailer, who had been asleep, awoke and was about to kill himself, but Paul shouted, "Do not harm yourself, for we are all here" (Acts 16:16-28).

That opened the door for Paul to tell the message of Jesus to the jailer, and he and his household were baptized (Acts 16:27-34).

Other Biblical References —

Paul told the Christians at Thessalonica how they had "suffered and been shamefully treated at Philippi" (1 Thessalonians 2:2).

Paul and Timothy wrote an encouraging letter to the Christians at Philippi (Philippians 1:1).

Archaeology in Philippi —

Modern archaeological work began in the last half of the 1800s. In 1860, Georges Perrot published an archaeological description based on his visit to the site in 1856.

In 1861, archaeologist Léon Heuzey and the architect Honoré Daumet of the French Mission Archéologique de Macédoine conducted a more thorough investigation.

In 1914, excavations were begun by the École française d'Athènes, but World War I interrupted this process. They were resumed in 1930 and continued until 1937.

The Archaeological Society of Athens, the Greek Archaeological

Service, and the University of Thessalonica excavated at different times from 1958 to 1978.

When we were there April 21, 2024, we saw the work the Ministry of Culture is currently undertaking. The Ministry is managing two large archaeological projects at Philippi. The value of these projects is €3,700,000 — almost US$4,000,000. The first project will create a new western entrance so that guests are oriented to the ancient road network. The second pursues additional restoration of Basilica B.

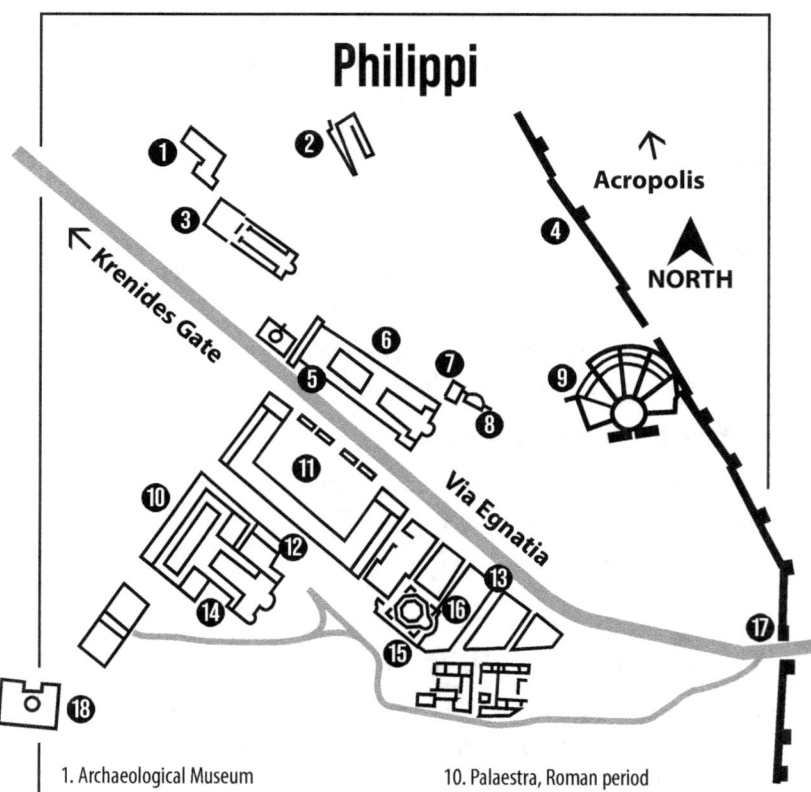

Philippi

Acropolis

NORTH

Krenides Gate

Via Egnatia

1. Archaeological Museum
2. Sanctuary of the Egyptian gods, Roman period
3. Basilica C, 6th century
4. City Walls, 4th century BC to Byzantine period
5. Traditional prison of Paul
6. Basilica A, 6th century
7. Sanctuary of Silvanus, Roman period
8. Sanctuary of Artemis, Roman period
9. Theatre, 4th century BC to Roman period

10. Palaestra, Roman period
11. Forum. Roman period
12. Commercial Agora, Roman period
13. Balneum (bath), Early Christian period
14. Basilica B, 6th century
15. Octagon church, 4th - 6th century
16. Bishop's palace
17. Gate of Neapolis, 4th century BC
18. Roman Villa

Sites To See —

Since 1957, various events have been held in this ancient theatre including classical drama, contemporary plays, dances, concerts, poetry recitations, and exhibitions.

The Theatre —

41.0128505, 24.2867033 / 41° 0' 46.262" N   24° 17' 12.132" E

This 4th century BC theatre was probably built by Philip II of Macedon. The Romans redesigned it in the 2nd and 3rd centuries to host their games. Today, it is used for theatrical and musical performances during the summer.

Basilica A —

41.0129761, 24.2844951 / 41° 0' 46.714" N   24° 17' 4.182" E

This large, 3-aisled basilica is just west of the theatre and was constructed about the end of the 5th century.

Prison of Paul —

41.0133035, 24.2835964 / 41° 0' 47.893" N   24° 17' 0.947" E

This is the traditional site of where Paul was cast into prison in Philippi. Some question whether or not this is the site, but it gives a perspective of what a prison might have been like.

Basilica C —

41.0141058, 24.2832983 / 41° 0′ 50.781″ N   24° 16′ 59.874″ E

This 3-aisle basilica probably dates from the 6th century.

Via Egnatia —

Within the ancient city of Philippi is a section of the Via Egnatia. This marble portion runs from southeast to northwest alongside the Roman forum. It shows grooves in the pavement that were made by chariots.

Pictured (above, left) are the remains of Basilica B with its large baptistry in the foreground. Numerous crosses and Christian symbols (above right) are around Philippi.

Roman Forum —

41.0126057, 24.2835633 / 41° 0′ 45.381″ N   24° 17′ 0.828″ E

There are many ruins in this area that was the administrative center of Philippi during the time of Roman rule. Remnants of buildings, columns, and monuments are found in the area.

Basilica B —

41.0118938, 24.2827974 / 41° 0′ 42.818″ N   24° 16′ 58.071″ E

This basilica dates back to about 550. At one time it was covered by a dome supported by large pillars. The structure was designed to rival major churches in cities such as Constantinople. It features a large immersion baptistry.

The Basilica of Paul —

41.0115872, 24.2845073 / 41° 0′ 41.714″ N   24° 17′ 4.226″ E

Built around 343, this building was probably a small prayer house. There is a mosaic in the pavement dedicating it to the apostle Paul.

The Octagon Church —

41.0115906, 24.2844009 / 41° 0' 41.726" N   24° 17' 3.843" E

The Octagon Church was built upon the ruins of the Basilica of Paul. It contains a cruciform shaped baptistry. Nearby is the Bishop's Palace.

This mosaic (above) notes the dedication of the Basilica of Paul. Paul's name is in yellow and is the first word on the bottom line.

The Octagon church (top right) was built on top of the Basilica of Paul.

To the right is a later church in which leaders sat in the front tiered section.

To the left is a cruciform shaped immersion baptistry that is in the Octagon church.

Reflections ...

When the apostle Paul was in a Roman prison, he wrote a letter to the Christians at Philippi. It is filled with joy, thanksgiving, comfort, and hope along with admonitions and exhortations. It is filled with inspirational quotes, comforting devotional thoughts, and challenging sermon messages.

He pointed to the example of Jesus Christ, and he bowed his head in prayer to the Father.

Right in the middle of the letter, Paul stated his deepest desires:
1) to know Him [Jesus Christ];
2) to know the power of His resurrection;
3) to know the fellowship of His suffering; and
4) to be conformed to His death (Philippians 3:10).

You and I may agree with the first two desires, but it is really hard for most of us to have a yearning for suffering and death by crucifixion. Yet, Paul said he wanted this "that by any means possible I may attain the resurrection from the dead" (Philippians 3:11).

He then stated, "Brothers, join in imitating me, and keep your eyes on those who walk according to the example you have in us" (Philippians 3:17).

Paul understood the ultimate goal. Do we?

Lydia's Baptismal Site

41.0207567, 24.2763753 / 41° 1' 14.724" N 24° 16' 34.951" E

Less than a mile north of ancient Philippi is the traditional site of the baptism of Lydia. Located on the River Zygaktis, it has a nice seating area and a finished baptismal pool.

Close by is an octagonal Greek Orthodox Church. This small chapel is filled with mosaics, icons, stained glass windows, and colorful frescos that tell the story of Paul teaching and baptizing Lydia along with the story of the jailer's conversion.

The River Zygaktis is a beautiful flowing peaceful river which provides a nice place for a devotional.

Below are photos of the Greek Orthodox Church. The entrance foyer has a large mosaic depicting Paul's second missionary journey. This section shows his travels from Troas to Neapolis to Philippi to Thessalonica. The bottom photo is the section of the ceiling showing the open jail doors and the jailer kneeling before Paul and Silas.

Chapter 9

Amphipolis – Home of the Lion

40.8252796, 23.8488056 / 40° 49′ 31.007″ N 23° 50′ 55.700″ E

Amphipolis was originally a village founded by people of Thrace and was named Ennea Hodoi, which means "nine roads." It became an Athenian colony in 437 BC when Hagnon captured it.

It was given the name Amphipolis which means "around the city." This name came from the fact that it sits in the bend of the Strymonas (Strymon / Struma) River. The city is about three miles from the Aegean Sea.

During the Second Peloponnesian War, Brasidas, a Spartan commander, conquered Amphipolis in 424 BC. He did this by allowing anyone staying to keep their property, and he allowed anyone who wanted to leave to do so.

When the Second Battle of Amphipolis took place in 422 BC, Brasidas addressed the soldiers and stated, "Bear in mind that the three virtues of a good soldier are zeal in battle, sense of honor, and obedience to the leaders… and I will reveal that I will conduct myself in action following the advice I give to my comrades."

Brasidas was wounded in battle, but before he died, he learned he had been victorious. He was buried in the agora of Amphipolis. The citizens honored him with annual games and later named him the city's founder.

Thucydides was an Athenian general who had been tasked with defending Amphipolis in 424 BC. However, he arrived after Brasidas had triumphed in his quest.

Thucydides was also a historian who believed the Peloponnesian War was an important turning point in history, so he wrote *History of the Peloponnesian War*.

Today, Amphipolis is a city of about 200 people with the area having a population of about 10,000.

The man who conquers himself is greater than the one who conquers a thousand men in battle.

I think the two things most opposed to good counsel are haste and passion; haste usually goes hand in hand with folly, passion with coarseness and narrowness of mind.

Men who are capable of real action first make their plans and then go forward without hesitation while their enemies have still not made up their minds.

I am more afraid of our own blunders than of the enemy's devices.

What was happening was democracy in name, but in fact the domination of the leading man.

Most people, in fact, will not take the trouble in finding out the truth, but are much more inclined to accept the first story they hear.

My work is not a piece of writing designed to meet the needs of an immediate public, but was done to last for ever.

— Thucydides, *History of the Peloponnesian War*

Archaeology in Amphipolis

The site of Amphipolis was discovered by archaeologists during the 19th century, but it was only after World War II that excavations began in earnest.

Digs have discovered a necropolis, basilicas, a bridge, the acropolis, villas, tombs, and the city wall. The most recent excavations have taken place since 2019 under the direction of Dr. Dimitria Malamidou along with Dr. Dimitrios Damaskos.

The Lion of Amphipolis

40.8030691, 23.8425449 / 40° 48' 11.049" N   23° 50' 33.162" E

As Paul and his companions traveled through Amphipolis when headed to Thessalonica, they may have seen the magnificent Lion of Amphipolis. However, we don't have any indication that Paul preached here, stayed here, or even saw the Lion.

Dating from the 4th century BC, the Lion of Amphipolis was originally located on the Great Tomb at Amphipolis and honored Laomedon of Mytilene, one of Alexander the Great's generals. The Lion is almost 18 feet tall, and it is over 26 feet tall when including its base.

During the First Balkan War, October 1912 to May 1913, Greek soldiers discovered parts of the Lion on the banks of the Strymonas (Strymon / Struma) River having been broken into several pieces. During World War 1, British soldiers discovered more of the Lion.

In the 1930s, while draining part of Lake Kerkini, large pieces of the marble Lion were found. Reconstruction of the lion began in 1937, and it stands today close to where it was found.

The Lion is just a little south of the archaeological ruins of the city of Amphipolis.

Chapter 10

Kandylakia – The Roadside Shrines

As we travel through Greece, we will see small roadside shrines known as kandylakia. They may be made of wood, concrete, stone, or metal. They reflect a variety of shapes and designs. Some are elaborate; others are simple. They may be along a country road or in a bustling city.

Some are there for the same reasons we see crosses along roadways in the US: there was a death there. But Greeks also place them as an expressions of thanksgiving for lives spared, a call to slow down and rest, or an invitation to prayer.

The little shrines often house an icon of a saint, a votive candle, or some other item of remembrance or worship. Many times the individual who established the shrine or the person's family pays a visit on the anniversary of the event which led to its placement.

Chapter 11

Apollonia – Mentioned in Passing

40.6394384, 23.4870046 / 40° 38′ 21.978″ N 23° 29′ 13.217″ E

Paul continued his journey from Philippi to Thessalonica and passed through Apollonia, which means "Belonging to Apollo." Located on the south side of Lake Bolbe (Límni Vólvi), Apollonia is on the Via Egnatia about halfway between Amphipolis and Thessalonica.

While we have no indication that Paul preached in Apollonia, Dr. John Brown of Haddington, Scotland, in his work, *Brown's Dictionary of Bible Words and Places* wrote, "A modern monument in Apollonia, written in both Greek and English, says, 'Here Took [Place] St. Paul's Speech.' The inscription also includes the text of Acts 17:1. The plaque is located on the side of a very small hill." The plaque still stands today.

Brown also recorded that Caesar Augustus learned Greek in Apollonia.

— PLAQUE LOCATION —

40.6432367, 23.4889955 / 40° 38′ 35.652″ N 23° 29′ 20.384″ E

Dr. John Brown of Haddington, Scotland, (1722-1787) was a Scottish minister, divinity professor, and author. After hearing him preach at North Berwick, David Hume said he preached "as if he were conscious that Christ was at his elbow."

Brown preached at Haddington for 36 years.

Chapter 12

Thessalonica – Faith After Rejection

40.6378108, 22.9457578 / 40° 38′ 16.119″ N 22° 56′ 44.728″ E

In 315 BC, Cassander of Macedon founded the city of Thessalonica. He named it after his wife, Thessalonike, a Macedonian Greek princess. Thessalonike's father was Philip II of Macedon, and her half-brother was Alexander the Great. Legend has it that after Alexander's death, she became a mermaid who lived in the Aegean Sea.

Thessalonica is located about 25 miles southeast of Pella, the capital of the ancient kingdom of Macedonia, on the northwest corner of the Aegean Sea by the Thermaic Gulf.

The Kingdom of Macedonia fell in 168 BC and became a Roman client state. In 148 BC, it became the Roman province of Macedonia.

During this time, the almost 700-mile long Via Egnatia was built. This ancient road connected Roman provinces from Dyrrachium on the Adriatic Sea (modern day Durrës, Albania) to Byzantium (modern day Istanbul, Türkiye) on the Bosphorous Strait.

The iconic White Tower sits on the coastline and can be seen from quite a distance.

The road enhanced trade, and because it ran through Thessalonica, merchants had access to a seaport midway.

When writing his multi-volume *Geography*, Greek geographer and historian Strabo (64 BC – 21 AD), stated that Thessalonica was more populous than any other city in Macedonia (Book 7, Chapter 7, Section 4). It was to this city that the apostle Paul traveled on his second missionary journey.

Paul in Thessalonica (Acts 17:1-10) —

As Paul traveled through the area, he stopped at Thessalonica where there was a synagogue of the Jews.

For three Sabbaths, he went to the synagogue to discuss the Scriptures. He may have begun teaching in Isaiah 53 as Philip did when he taught the Ethiopian — we don't know. But we can be assured that he began with Scripture and prophecy which led to his teaching about the resurrected Christ.

Because of his teaching from the Scriptures and the power of God, some believed. Among the believers were God-fearing Greeks and leading women. However, the Jews were jealous; they formed a mob; they dragged Jason and other believers before the city authorities; they accused them of saying there was another king besides Caesar.

Aristotle Square features a beautiful floral clock. Thessaloniki boasts a variety of architectural styles including Byzantine, neoclassical, eclecticism, and art deco.

After this uproar, the brethren sent Paul and those traveling with him away to Berea. But this would not be the end of the story. We'll follow up when we visit Berea.

Also remember, even though Paul was run out of the city, a strong church would later find its place in Thessalonica.

Other Biblical References —

◆ The Bereans were more noble than those in Thessalonica (Acts 17:11).

◆ Jews from Thessalonica learned Paul went to Berea, and they went there to stir up the crowd (Acts 17:13).

◆ The Christians in Philippi helped support Paul when he was in Thessalonica (Philippians 4:17).

◆ Demas deserted Paul and went to Thessalonica (2 Timothy 4:10).

◆ Paul wrote two letters to the Christians in Thessalonica: 1 Thessalonians and 2 Thessalonians.

Sites To See —

Ancient Agora —

40.6378724, 22.9456856 / 40° 38' 16.341" N   22° 56' 44.468" E

In 1963, while breaking ground for a new government building, a 1st century agora was discovered. Originally constructed by the Greeks, the Romans had later added a second level.

The odeon (left) sits on the eastern side of the Roman forum and could seat about 200 people.

The ruins of the Roman agora (right) give insight into the lives of the people during the time Paul preached in Thessalonica.

Another area of ruins from the Roman agora is pictured on the left.

Arch of Galerius —

40.6322426, 22.9517539 / 40° 37' 56.073" N   22° 57' 6.314" E

Roman emperor Galerius commissioned the arch to celebrate his victorious campaign against the Persians on 298 AD.

White Tower —

40.6264629, 22.9483848 / 40° 37' 35.266" N   22° 56' 54.185" E

The imposing White Tower was originally built by the Ottomans as a fortress in the 15th century.

Religion in Thessaloniki —

With a population of about 815,000, about 90% of the people identify as Greek Orthodox. The remainder are as follows: Other Christians, 3%; Islam, 2%; Other Religions, 1%; Unaffiliated, 4%.

Reflections ...

When Paul went into Thessalonica, he went to the synagogue as was his custom. He met the people where they were in their faith walk with God.

Although Paul had opposition in this city and may have wanted to write it off as a defeat, God brought victory by His power in His time.

When Paul wrote his first letter to these Christians, he stated, "We give thanks to God always for all of you, constantly mentioning you in our prayers, remembering before our God and Father your work of faith and labor of love and steadfastness of hope in our Lord Jesus Christ" (1 Thessalonians 1:2-3).

Perhaps the end of chapter 1 gives more definition to these three points:

Work of Faith —

"For not only has the word of the Lord sounded forth from you in Macedonia and Achaia, but your faith in God has gone forth everywhere, so that we need not say anything" (1:8).

Labor of Love —

"For they themselves report concerning us the kind of reception we had among you, and how you turned to God from idols to serve the living and true God" (1:9).

Steadfastness of Hope —

"and to wait for his Son from heaven, whom he raised from the dead, Jesus who delivers us from the wrath to come" (1:10).

May we all receive such a great commendation.

Chapter 13

Pella – Where Alexander Was Born

40.7619616, 22.5198816 / 40° 45' 43.062" N 22° 31' 11.574" E

About 24 miles northwest of Thessaloniki is Pella, the city where Alexander the Great was born in 356 BC. As a child growing up in Pella, Alexander was tutored by the famous philosopher Aristotle.

Located near the Vardar (Axios) River, the area shows signs of human habitation as early as the Neolithic period. Pella was founded in the 4th century BC by King Archelaus, and it quickly became the cultural and political center in Macedon. Its impressive royal palace reflected the wealth and power of the Macedonian monarchy. During the reign of Philip II of Macedon, Pella flourished as a hub of artistic and intellectual activity.

Archaeology in Pella —

In 1953, Athanasios Kondrouphis, a local school teacher and amateur archaeologist, came across the ruins of Pella by chance.

The city's palace, which has been excavated and partially restored, is believed to be the very place where Alexander spent his formative years. The palace complex, with its impressive architecture and stunning mosaics, is a testament to the wealth and power of the Macedonian kingdom during its heyday. The ruins include a throne room, living quarters, and a courtyard.

Another significant archaeological discovery at Pella is the ancient agora. Archaeologists have also unearthed a plethora of artifacts that offer a glimpse into the daily lives of Pella's ancient inhabitants.

Sites To See —

In March 2010, the Pella Archaeological Museum opened. Exhibits include the large marble head of Alexander the great, beautiful floor mosaics, coins, and various objects of stone, metal, and ceramic. The museum gives you the opportunity to understand the daily activities of the city.

Less than a mile south of the museum is the Pella Archaeological Park. There you will see Dionysos Mosaic Place, the Helen House, the public baths, mosaics, the forum, columns, and various ruins.

Chapter 14

Vergina – Home of Ancient Aigai

The modern city of Vergina was established in 1922. It is the site of ancient Aigai which was the original capital of Macedonia.

The Palace of Aigai was constructed by Philip II of Macedon in the 4th century BC and covers an area of 160,000 square feet. It, along with the Parthenon, are said to be the two most significant structures of classical Greece.

Philip II was assassinated in the theatre at Aigai by one of his seven bodyguards in 336 BC. His son Alexander the Great was crowned king of Macedon at the Palace of Aigai. He was 20 years old and immediately eliminated possible rivals to the throne. The palace was destroyed by the Romans in 148 BC.

The area was an important population center as early as 1000 BC.

Discovering the Tomb —

On November 8, 1977, Dr. Manolis Andronikos made his greatest archaeological discovery when he found a cluster of royal tombs — one of which belonged to Philip II of Macedon, the father of Alexander the Great.

Because Andronikos entered Philip II of Macedon's tomb from the top, the entrance was not damaged.

Andronicos had been excavating in the area of Vergina, Greece, for 40 years. Other tombs and artifacts had been discovered, but none matched the grandeur and importance of Philip II's tomb. Items of gold, silver, bronze, and ivory were discovered.

Within Philip II of Macedon's tomb was a golden larnax, a small burial chest. The symbol of the Macedonian royal family — a 16-pointed star — adorned its lid. Inside were cremated remains, a golden wreath, and an exquisitely designed helmet.

Philip II's ceremonial armor and shield (left) was discovered in his tomb.

The contents of the Golden Larnax (right) found in Philip II's tomb included a golden wreath.

A massive earthen mound — the Great Tumulus — covered these 4th century BC tombs and protected them from grave robbers. After the discovery, the archaeologists accessed the tombs by entering through the top of each tomb, thus keeping the magnificent facade intact.

Visiting Vergina —

Museum of the Royal Tombs of Aigai (Vergina) —

40.4874388, 22.3202566 / 40° 29' 14.780" N 22° 19' 12.924" E

In 1993, an underground museum at the site of the tombs was opened. You can see the undisturbed entrance of Philip II's tomb, his golden crown, and the intricately designed larnax. Displays include gold and ivory couches, beautiful frescoes, shields, and Macedonian body armor.

On the frieze of Tomb III's ante-chamber was this painting of a chariot race.

The Palace of Aigai —

40.4778629, 22.3223371 / 40° 28′ 40.306″N 22° 19′ 20.414″E

On January 7, 2024, the Palace of Aigai, which is just a few minutes south of the tombs, was opened after 16 years of excavation and restoration. The project was aided by members of the European Union and cost about $22,000,000. The Palace is a 160,000 square foot marvel. This is where Alexander the Great was crowned King of Macedon after his father's assassination.

Other sites in Vergina —

Also in Vergina are the Royal Burial Cluster of the Temenids, Burial Cluster of the Queens, Ancient Theatre of Aigai, Sanctuary of Eucleia, and Prehistoric Cemetery of Aigai — some of which are temporarily closed.

Impact on Christianity —

When Alexander the Great was spreading Greek culture, customs, and language, he did so to broaden his kingdom and for self glory. Depending on the source, he named somewhere between 20 and 70 cities after himself. Perhaps the most famous is Alexandria, Egypt.

Although he was conquering for Greece and himself, what he achieved served to advance another kingdom — the Kingdom of God. As we study Nebuchadnezzar's dream in Daniel 2 and Daniel's interpretation of it by the power of God (Daniel 2:28), we see the revelation of coming kingdoms. The approaching kingdoms included the kingdom of Greece (Daniel 8:21).

At the time of the birth of Jesus, the Greek language was common throughout much of the world. The New Testament was written in Greek. People could read the word of God.

May we remember that what we do today will impact — positively or negatively — the Kingdom of God.

Manolis Andronikos was born on October 23, 1919 in Prousa (modern day Bursa), in northern Türkiye — a little over two hours south of Istanbul.

He studied at Aristotle University of Thessaloniki and later at Oxford University.

Andronikos taught archaeology and excavated at several sites including Vergina. He died March 30, 1992.

Chapter 15

Berea – A Noble Beginning

40.5185018, 22.2000155 / 40° 31′ 6.606″ N   22° 12′ 0.056″ E

Ruins of the area of Berea go back to 700 BC although archaeological evidence points to human settlement as early as 1000 BC.

Thucydides gave a brief reference to Berea in *The History of the Peloponnesian War*. In 168 BC, Berea was the first city in Macedonia to be conquered by the Romans in the Battle of Pydna during the Third Macedonian War.

The Bema of Paul in Berea features exquisite mosaics with the left panel depicting his receiving the vision at Troas and the right panel showing his teaching in Berea. Below the center portrait of Paul are three marble steps believed to have come from a first century synagogue.

Paul in Berea —

After the uproar in Thessalonica, Paul traveled to Berea — a distance of about 46 miles. This was probably a 2- or 3-day journey.

Paul went to the synagogue in Berea, and many people believed. When the Jews in Thessalonica heard about this, they went to Berea to stir things up. They were so enraged with Paul and the message he was preaching — they had such uncontrollable anger — that they took a week off work just to complain!

The people at Berea were commended because they delved into the scriptures to verify what Paul was teaching. "Now these Jews were more noble than those in Thessalonica; they received the word with all eagerness, examining the Scriptures daily to see if these things were so" (Acts 17:11).

However, because of the problem caused by the Jews from Thessalonica, some believers took Paul to the coast and on to Athens. Silas and Thomas stayed in Berea for a period of time.

Berea in the Bible —

Sopater the Berean traveled with Paul on part of his third missionary journey (Acts 20:4). This implies the possibility of Paul's visiting Berea on his third journey.

The Bema of Paul —

Just a short distance from Raktavin Square in downtown Berea is a small plaza with "The Bema of Saint Paul." It was built to commemorate his visits to Berea and is reputed to be at the location where he preached.

As you enter, there is a stately bronze statue of the apostle on the right that was donated by the Moscow Patriarchate and the Russian Academy of Arts. Across the small plaza are three stunning mosaics. One depicts Paul's vision of seeing the man from Macedonia urging him "Come over to Macedonia and help us" (Acts 16:9). In the center is the apostle Paul. The right-hand mosaic pictures his preaching in Berea.

Below the center mosaic of the apostle are three marble steps taken from a 1st century synagogue where it is believed that Paul preached.

Reflections ...

Although the Bereans were stated to be more noble than the folks in Thessalonica because they searched the scriptures, we don't have evidence that the church there was as strong as the church in Thessalonica — a city from which he had to flee and home to people who followed Paul to agitate his ministry. The only other reference in the Bible to Berea or anyone from Berea is Sopater (Acts 20:4).

Not only must we be people who search the scriptures, we must be people who are faithful to the scriptures.

Chapter 16

Mount Olympus – Impressive Height

40.0859571, 22.3581841 / 40° 5' 9.446" N 22° 21' 29.463" E

Mount Olympus is the highest mountain in Greece with an elevation of 9,572 feet. It is located about 10 miles from the Thermaic Gulf of the Aegean Sea. It is about 50 miles southwest of Thessaloniki and 162 miles north northwest of Athens as the crow flies.

In 1938, Mount Olympus became Greece's first national park.

Mount Olympus, according to Greek mythology, is home to the Greek gods. It is a popular hiking destination with trails that are easy, medium, and difficult. The area offers a variety of other activities including paragliding, rafting, and mountain biking.

Its overall elevation is not as high as the 58 fourteeners in Colorado. However, when measuring its height from its prominence, Mount Olympus is higher than all Colorado fourteeners except one. Prominence is the distance of the lowest area around the mountain to its summit.

Colorado's highest mountain is Mount Elbert. It is 14,440 feet high, and its prominence is 9,093 feet. Mount Olympus is 9,472 feet in elevation with a prominence is 7,720 feet. Pikes Peak, one of Colorado's best-known mountains, is 14,115 feet high, but its prominence is 5,530 feet.

The Monastery of Holy Trinity

Chapter 17

Meteora – Unique Geological Formations

Some tours take time to go to Kalabaka, Greece, and see the Meteora Monasteries.

The pillars at Meteora stand out because of their unique and intriguing geological structure as they emerge from the valley. As you view them, you may think you are on another planet. In 1989, Meteora was listed as a UNESCO World Heritage Site.

The tallest of these pillars reaches over 1,000 feet into the sky.

In about the 9th or 10th century, Orthodox Christian monks were the first to ascend these cliffs to find quiet and isolate themselves. Nilos began organizing the monks in about the 12th century. In the 14th century, Athanasios established the first Meteora monastery on the second-highest rock. At one point there were 24 active monasteries; today there are six.

The Monastery of Holy Trinity —
39.7131717, 21.6358118 / 39° 42′ 47.418″ N 21° 38′ 8.922″ E

The Monastery of Holy Trinity (Agia Triada) at Meteora was built in 1458 and is one of the most photographed pillars in the area. At the same time, it's the most difficult to reach. Those who will attempt to reach it will be rewarded with the panoramic view of the surroundings which is simply captivating!

You may recognize this monastery as it was featured in the James Bond movie, *For Your Eyes Only*. Bond, played by actor Roger Moore, scaled the face of the dangerous cliff. This monastery has the most dramatic location of the various monasteries at Meteora.

Chapter 18

Delphi – Home of the Oracle

38.4819085, 22.5028324 / 38° 28′ 54.871″ N 22° 30′ 10.197″ E

According to myths, Zeus, the sky and thunder god in ancient Greek religion and mythology, sent two eagles from the opposite ends of the earth, and they met in what we know as Delphi, Greece. Zeus marked the spot with a sacred stone. Thus Delphi became the navel — or center — of the earth. Zeus then placed the Omphalos there.

The remaining columns of the Temple of Apollo at Delphi stand tall against the horizon.

Delphi was developed in the 8th century BC and is located about 75 miles northwest of Athens as the crow flies. Situated on the slopes of Mount Parnassus, Delphi was a religious sanctuary dedicated to Apollo who was a Greek god of just about everything including music, poetry, art, archery, healing, prophecy…

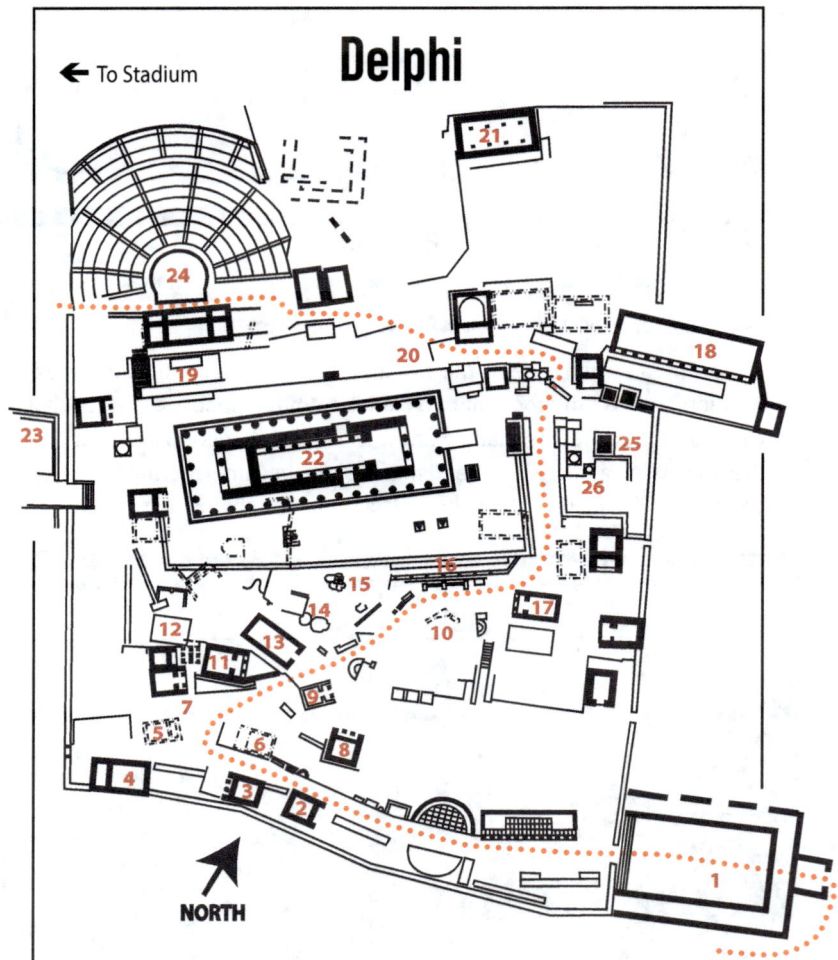

Delphi

← To Stadium

NORTH

1. The Roman Agora
2. The Treasury of the Sikyonians
3. The Treasury of the Siphnians
4. The Treasury of the Thebans
5. The Treasury of the Boeotians
6. The Treasury of the Megarians
7. Navel Stone (Omphalos)
8. Unknown Treasury
9. The Treasury of the Knidians
10. The "Halos"
11. The Treasury of the Athenians
12. The Asclepieion
13. The Bouleuterion
14. The Rock of the Sibylle
15. The Sphinx of the Naxians
16. The Stoa of the Athenians
17. The Treasury of the Corinthians
18. The Stoa of Attalos
19. The Offering of Krateros
20. Kassotis Spring
21. The Hall of the Knidians
22. The Temple of Apollo
23. The Great Stoa of the Aitolians
24. The Theatre
25. Chariot of the Rodians
26. Tripod of Plataea

Pythia was the high priestess of the Temple of Apollo at Delphi. She was believed to speak the word of Apollo and was known as the Oracle of Delphi. As important people of the world came to her for advice, she would take her place in the Temple of Apollo and utter unintelligible sounds — perhaps while in a hallucinogenic trance — which the priests would then interpret. This brought large sums of money to Delphi.

Sometimes called the "Stone of Pythia," French archaeologists removed this stone from the floor of a small sunken room at Delphi.

There is no evidence that the apostle Paul visited Delphi, but he certainly would have been aware of what took place here. Perhaps, while speaking on Mars Hill in Athens about the gods the Athenians worshipped, he also had this site in mind.

When Paul and Silas were in Philippi, they were approached by a slave girl who had a spirit of divination (Acts 16:16). The Greek word for divination is πύθων — "Python" — and it means python. It was Apollo who, according to Greek mythology, slew Python — a giant serpent/dragon — so he could build his temple at Delphi from which Pythia spoke words of divination.

Yahweh prohibits His followers from being involved with witchcraft, divination, and such (Leviticus 19:31; Deuteronomy 18:9-14). When Paul was in Ephesus on his third journey, people who became followers of Jesus Christ and had practiced sorcery "brought their books together and burned them in the sight of all" (Acts 19:19).

Sites To See —

As you enter ancient Delphi, you see the **Roman Agora** where people would buy and sell. Continuing down the path, you come to the Navel of the Earth sculpture, also known as the Omphalos of Delphi.

The **Athenian Treasury** was constructed in the 6th century BC to receive offerings made to Apollo and the oracle. Just a little distance from the treasury is the **Stoa of the Athenians**. This ancient portico was constructed about 475 BC.

The Treasury of the Athenians was constructed using a semitranslucent pure white marble from the Greek island of Paros.

As you proceed up the hill, you come to the **Serpent Column**, the Tripod of the Plataeans. This sacrificial structure commemorated Greeks who fought and defeated the Persians at the Battle of Plataea (479 BC). This is a reconstructed column as the original is in Istanbul.

The original Serpent Column was taken to Constantinople (Istanbul) by Constantine. This replica was completed in 2015.

Standing out among the ruins is the **Temple of Apollo** with its Doric design. Originally constructed around the 7th century BC, it was later destroyed in a fire. In the 6th century BC it was rebuilt. In 373 BC, it was destroyed by an earthquake but was rebuilt again in 330 BC. In 390 AD, Roman Emperor Theodosius I ordered the destruction of all pagan temples, and the Temple of Apollo was destroyed.

Adjacent to the northeast entrance to the Temple of Apollo is the **Pillar of Prusias II**. It was built in 182 BC to honor King Prusias of Bithynia.

Located uphill from the Temple of Apollo is the **Ancient Theatre of Delphi**. It dates back to the 4th century BC and could seat nearly 5,000 people.

The **Stadium of Delphi** can seat 6,500 people and was built to host the Pythian Games. The games ranked second only to the Olympics and were held every four years to honor Apollo.

Gallio Inscription

In the early 1900s, a French excavation team discovered several fragments of a copy of a letter from Emperor Claudius to the city of Delphi. The letter, which would have been written in 52, references "my friend and proconsul L. Iunius Gallio."

While Paul was in Corinth, the Jews charged Paul with "persuading the people to worship God in ways contrary to the law." They took him to the place of judgment — the bema — and it was Gallio who responded. Gallio was proconsul of Achaia at that time (Acts 18:12). Because of Gallio's short tenure as proconsul, this places Paul in Corinth in 52.

Archaeological Museum of Delphi —

38.4802944, 22.4998970 / 38° 28′ 49.060″ N   22° 29′ 59.629″ E

This magnificent museum holds an abundance of artifacts from ancient Delphi including fragments of statues from the Treasury of the Mammalians, the Altar from the sanctuary of Athena Pronaia, metopes from the Tholos and other buildings, a copy of the on-halos of the earth, and bronze statuettes.

Other impressive items are a large sphinx of Naxos, the frieze from the treasury of Siphnos, and the Charioteer of Delphi. Before you exit the building, you will see the Delphi Inscription.

The Tholos of Delphi is an intriguing site. However, too many groups just stop on the highway for a quick photo — if they stop at all. — PHOTO BY DALE W. MANOR

Tholos of Delphi —

38.4801685, 22.5078934 / 38° 28′ 48.607″ N 22° 30′ 28.416″ E

Just down the road from Delphi are the remains of the Tholos of Delphi which dates from about 380–370 BC. This circular temple shares its site with the Doric-styled Temple of Athena Pronaia which was constructed about the 7th century BC.

Reflections ...

As he was nearing the end of his life, Joshua called all of God's people together at Shechem (Joshua 24). He then reviewed how God had continually provided for and delivered His people generation after generation after generation.

Throughout the centuries, God's people had been tempted to follow other ways of life and to seek direction from other sources.

Joshua then challenged them, "And if it is evil in your eyes to serve the LORD, choose this day whom you will serve, whether the gods your fathers served in the region beyond the River, or the gods of the

Amorites in whose land you dwell. But as for me and my house, we will serve the LORD" (Joshua 24:15).

This has always been the choice: Yahweh or other gods; Yahweh or mediums; Yahweh or sorcerers; Yahweh or other philosophies; Yahweh or my own will…

This was a big problem with King Saul, and it was why he lost his kingdom. He never got "self" out of the way in his relationship with the almighty God.

Perhaps this scripture is God's most comprehensive command on sorcery, "When you come into the land that the LORD your God is giving you, you shall not learn to follow the abominable practices of those nations. There shall not be found among you anyone who burns his son or his daughter as an offering, anyone who practices divination or tells fortunes or interprets omens, or a sorcerer or a charmer or a medium or a necromancer or one who inquires of the dead, for whoever does these things is an abomination to the LORD. And because of these abominations the LORD your God is driving them out before you. You shall be blameless before the LORD your God, for these nations, which you are about to dispossess, listen to fortune-tellers and to diviners. But as for you, the LORD your God has not allowed you to do this" (Deuteronomy 18:9-14).

Yahweh has always been opposed to sorcery, witchcraft, and idolatry. Why? These ways of life lead people down a path of destruction, selfishness, evil, and conflict.

You and I have been created in the image of God for a purpose-filled life. His love for us is eternal, and He gave His Son — His only begotten Son — to die a cruel death on a rugged cross so that we might have eternal life with Him. And thank God — Jesus was raised from the dead victorious over sin, death, and Satan!

It is at the name of Jesus that every knee will bow (Philippians 2:10). It was Jesus who said, "The thief comes only to steal and kill and destroy. I came that they may have life and have it abundantly" (John 10:10). And the life He offers is eternal.

Just as Joshua challenged the people to be faithful to God, we face the same challenges. May we answer as Joshua did, "But as for me and my house, we will serve the LORD" (Joshua 24:15).

Chapter 19

Athens – Paul's Challenging Sermon

37.9715084, 23.7258053 / 37° 58′ 17.430″ N 23° 43′ 32.899″ E

Often referred to as the "cradle of western civilization," Athens was named after Athena, the ancient Greek goddess of wisdom.

The magnificence of the Acropolis of Athens presents a striking view as people enter the city. It would have been more so during the time the apostle Paul visited Athens. This photo was taken looking toward the east. — PHOTO BY DALE W. MANOR

The city of Athens has a long and storied history. Believed to have been continuously inhabited since about 5000 BC, the first recorded history of Athens began about 1400 BC when it became an important center in Mycenaean civilization. Indications are that a Mycenaean palace was located on the Acropolis.

The Golden Age of Athens spanned from the 5th century to the 4th century BC. It was during this time that both the Parthenon and the

Temple of Athena Nike were built. The city attracted scholars, artists, and philosophers from all around the Mediterranean world.

The influence of Athens began to dim during the Peloponnesian War which took place from 431-404 BC. The Spartans gained influence during this period.

In 338 BC, Athens came under the rule of Philip II of Macedon. Alexander the Great followed his father in ruling the area.

Mars Hill is a rather nondescript rock, but it is where Paul preached his most famous sermon. This photo from the Acropolis gives a good view of Mars Hill.

Paul in Athens —

Paul's arrival in Athens may not have coincided with his planned itinerary — if he had anything close to a planned itinerary. Because of repeated opposition from the agitators from Thessalonica, brethren sent him away from Berea, and he came to Athens by sea. At this point, he didn't have any companions with him.

He walked around Athens and saw all the idols. He reasoned with people in the synagogue. He wound up on the Areopagus (Mars Hill) because some of the philosophers wanted to know what he was preaching.

It was because of these interruptions in his life that Paul preached what is probably his most famous sermon. A few were converted to

Jesus Christ, but only two are named: Dionysius the Areopagite and a woman named Damaris (Acts 17:34).

As we look at this most stirring and challenging sermon, we might anticipate a large number of people becoming Christians and a strong church being established in Athens. But that is not the case.

Noel Whitlock, Frank Wheeler, and Kenneth Mills stand at the base of Mars Hill and in front of a bronze plaque which contains Paul's sermon. — PHOTO BY KAY MILLS

Other Biblical References —

Athens is only mentioned one other time in the New Testament, and that is 1 Thessalonians 3:1-2, where Paul wrote, "Therefore when we could bear it no longer, we were willing to be left behind at Athens alone, and we sent Timothy, our brother and God's coworker in the gospel of Christ, to establish and exhort you in your faith."

This apparently references Paul's arriving alone in the city of Athens having left Timothy and Silas in Berea. At the time Paul was preaching his famous sermon on Mars Hill, Timothy may well have been teaching and encouraging the saints in Thessalonica.

When Paul arrived in Athens, it had lost its standing in the world as the leading cultural and commercial center.

Today, Athens is the capital of Greece, and it once again is a leader culturally, commercially, and educationally. There are 14 universities in Athens. Athens is also home to 19 archaeological institutes with the French School at Athens being the oldest, having been established in 1846. The population of Athens is about 650,000, but the population reaches 3,000,000 when including the urban area.

As we visit the cities which Paul visited and the respective archaeological sites, Athens is unique in that it is the only archaeological site surrounded by a modern-day city.

Athens

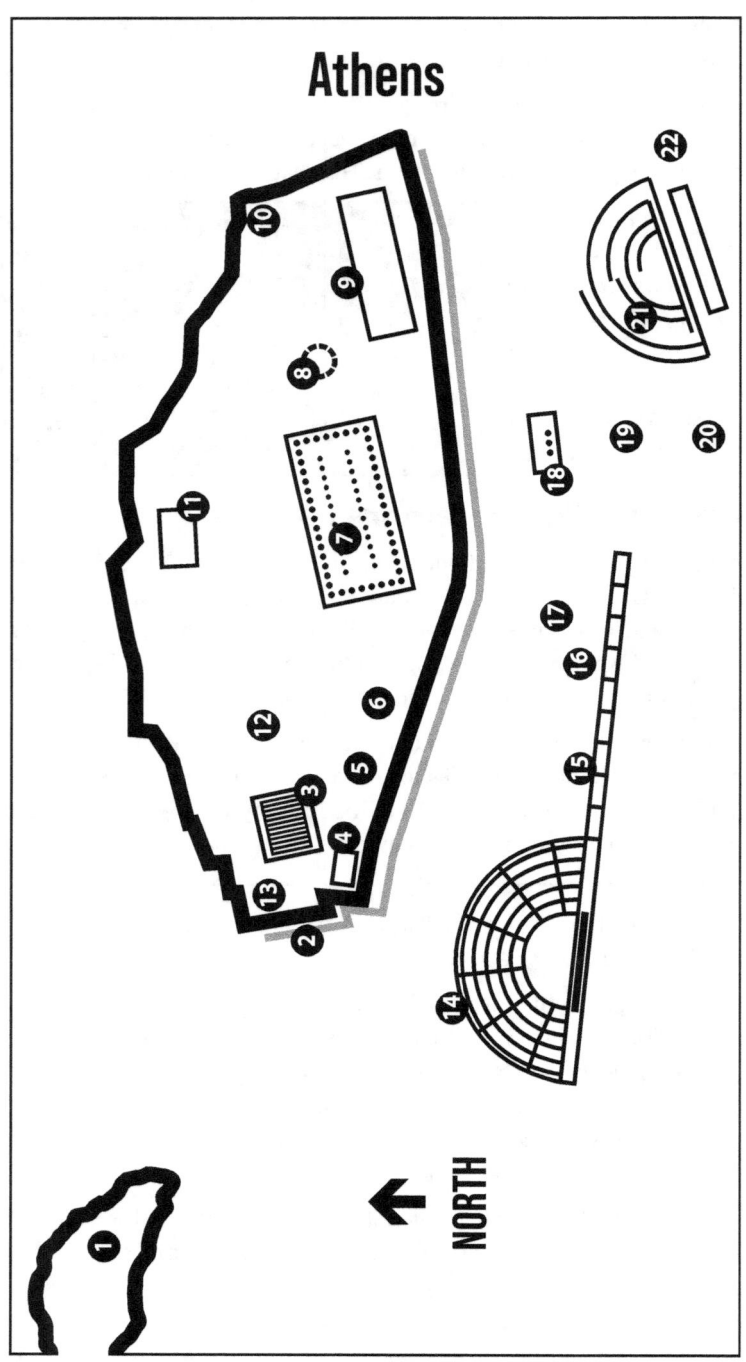

NORTH

As you look over the south ledge of the Acropolis, you have a good overhead view of the Theatre of Dionysus on the south slope. It was rediscovered in 1765, and German archaeologist Wilhelm Dörpfeld undertook some restoration work in the 1800s.

In the top of the photo and across Dionysiou Areopagitou Street, you see the angular shape of the modern Acropolis Museum which was opened June 20, 2009. More than 4,250 objects are exhibited in this 150,000 square foot building.

Sites for Athens Map

1. Mars Hill / The Areopagus

The Acropolis —

2. The Beulé Gate
3. Propylaea
4. Temple of Athena Nike
5. Sanctuary of Artemis Brauronia
6. Chalkotheke
7. Parthenon
8. Temple of Rome & Augustus
9. Old Acropolis Museum
10. Greek Flag of Athens Acropolis
11. Erechtheion
12. Statue of Athena Promachus (Base)
13. Monument of Agrippa

South Slope —

14. Odeon of Herodes Atticus
15. Stoa of Eumenes
16. Byzantine Cistern
17. Temple of Themis
18. Temple of Asklepios
19. Peripatos
20. The Choregic Monument of Nikes
21. Theatre of Dionysus
22. Chapel of Saint George Alexandrinos

Sites To See —

When one visits Athens, the central focus is the Acropolis and the temples on it. Although Lycabettus Hill is the highest point in Athens, it is the imposing Acropolis and its surrounding area that lay claim to the city's history.

On the Acropolis —

Like many sites in Greece, the surface of the Acropolis is marble. Thus, it can be very slick. They have poured concrete over much of the surface in the past couple of years, and this is a better walking surface. However, periodically they have small areas like a shallow bowl where the surface marble can be seen. As you walk across the Acropolis, be watchful for these places.

As you look to the entrance to the Acropolis, you see the Temple of Athena Nike and her four columns toward the right side. To the left is the 30-foot tall Pedestal of Agrippa in front of the north wing of the Propylaea. — PHOTO BY DALE W. MANOR

The Beulé Gate —

37.9716088, 23.7246351 / 37° 58′ 17.792″ N 23° 43′ 28.686″ E

This fortified gate leads to the Propylaea of the Acropolis of Athens. The stone used in its construction was from the Choragic Monument of Nikias which was built about 320 BC but was destroyed somewhere around the 3rd century AD.

Propylaea —

37.9717117, 23.7250347 / 37° 58′ 18.162″ N 23° 43′ 30.125″ E

This grand structure of marble buildings and majestic columns is the main entrance to the Acropolis.

Temple of Athena Nike —

37.9715521, 23.7249087 / 37° 58′ 17.588″ N 23° 43′ 29.671″ E

You may have seen this temple as you were approaching the Propylaea, but if not: Around the corner and to the right from the Propylaea is the Temple of Athena Nike which was completed in 420 BC. It was built using beautiful white Pentelic marble. The columns showcase the distinctive Ionic design.

Although much smaller than the Parthenon, the Temple of Athena Nike is impressive in her own right as she sits by the entrance to the Acropolis.

Sanctuary of Artemis Brauronia —

37.9714345, 23.7254910 / 37° 58′ 17.164″ N 23° 43′ 31.768″ E

The ruins of this sanctuary are located in the southwest corner of the Acropolis. The sanctuary was dedicated to Artemis Brauronia who is the protector of women in pregnancy and childbirth.

Chalkotheke —

37.9713576, 23.7257775 / 37° 58′ 16.887″ N 23° 43′ 32.799″ E

This building, which now lies in ruins, was built around 450 BC and believed to be a treasury. An inscription from around 353 BC lists various items — weapons, statuettes, and bronze vessels — which were housed in the building and believed to have been dedicated on the Acropolis to Athena.

Parthenon —
37.9715217, 23.7264604 / 37° 58′ 17.478″ N   23° 43′ 35.257″ E

This monumental structure is the central focus of the Acropolis. It was built to honor the Hellenic victory over Persia during the Greco-Persian Wars. Construction began in 447 BC and was completed in 432 BC.

When visiting the once-magnificent Parthenon, you see the cranes, scaffolding, and workers as the building is constantly undergoing repair and reconstruction.

The Parthenon uses both Doric and Ionic influences in its design and contains 46 outer columns and 23 inner columns. The temple is comprised of over 70,000 individual pieces with each being handcrafted for its specific placement.

In the late 5th century, the Parthenon became a Catholic church, Church of the Virgin Mary. It remained a Christian church building for about 1,000 years.

Exquisite carvings graced the Parthenon. From 1801 to 1803, Lord Elgin, a British nobleman and diplomat, removed many of the Parthenon Marbles, and they are currently housed in the British Museum. The legitimacy of their removal and relocation continues to be a point of contention between Great Britain and Greece.

Temple of Rome & Augustus —

37.9716670, 23.7273160 / 37° 58' 18.001" N   23° 43' 38.338" E

Standing about 75 feet east of the Parthenon are the remains of the Temple of Rome & Augustus. This temple was about 28 feet in diameter with nine columns of the ionic order. This circular temple was built at some point after 27 BC — possibly as late as 10 BC — when Octavian received the title Augustus. It pays tribute to Rome.

The following inscription was found in the 19th century:

The people [dedicate] to the goddess Roma and Caesar Augustus, being hoplite general Pammenes [son of] Zenon of Marathon, [also] priest of the goddess Roma and Augustus Savior on the acropolis, when the priestess of Athena Polias was Megiste daughter of Asklepides of Halai, under the archonship of Areios [son of] Dorion of Paiania.

Old Acropolis Museum —

37.9714775, 23.7275936 / 37° 58' 17.319" N   23° 43' 39.337" E

This museum was built in 1874 and closed in 2007, but its restrooms were still open when we were there in 2024.

The new **Acropolis Museum** opened June 20, 2009. It houses more than 4,250 items, and the entrance is on Dionysiou Areopagitou Street across from the south slope of the Acropolis. Its coordinates are 37.9685199, 23.7284754 / 37° 58' 6 672" N   23° 43' 42.511" E.

Greek Flag of Athens Acropolis —

37.9718633, 23.7279615 / 37° 58' 18.708" N   23° 43' 40.661" E

This easternmost point of the Acropolis is another great vantage point overlooking this magnificent city.

Erechtheion —

37.9721233, 23.7263904 / 37° 58' 19.644" N   23° 43' 35.005" E

The Erechtheion, also known as the Temple of Athena Polias, was erected in 421–406 BC. This ancient Greek Ionic temple was primarily dedicated to the goddess Athena.

It draws attention because of its use of Caryatids — a female statue or a support column shaped like a female — which support the roof of the south porch.

One of the more interesting buildings on the Acropolis is the Erechtheion because of its use of Caryatids (see photo below) in supporting the roof of its porch. — PHOTO BY DALE W. MANOR

Base of the Statue of Athena Promachus —

37.9718331, 23.7257266 / 37° 58' 18.599" N 23° 43' 32.616" E

The Statue of Athena Promachos was immense bronze statue by Pheidias. It was erected about 456 BC. It is reported that sailors as far away as Cape Sounion could see her gleaming helmet and spear. Byzantine Emperor Justinian I carried the statue to Constantinople in the 6th century. She was lost to other looters centuries later. All that remains is the base of the statue.

Pedestal of Agrippa —

37.9718015, 23.7248538 / 37° 58' 18.485" N 23° 43' 29.474" E

As you exit the Acropolis and head down the stairs, you come face-to-face with the Pedestal of Agrippa. It was built in 178 BC to honor Eumenes II of Pergamum after he won the chariot race in the Panathenaic Games. The monument is about 30 feet tall and was originally the base of a bronze four-horse chariot with riders.

The South Slope —

There are a few structures of interest on the south slope of the Acropolis. When you are on the south side of the Acropolis, you can look down and have an excellent view of the Odeon of Herodes Atticus. As with many sites in Athens, these range from excellent preservation/reconstruction condition to the evidence of a few visible ruins.

As you view the Odeon of Herodes Atticus from above, you get a glimpse of its grandeur.

Odeon of Herodes Atticus —

37.9707879, 23.7245745 / 37° 58′ 14.836″ N   23° 43′ 28.468″ E

This open-air theatre was completed in 161 and renovated in 1950. It seats 5,000 and is used for concerts and plays. Entrance is only allowed during a ticketed event.

Sanctuary of Asklepios —

37.9708098, 23.7268278 / 37° 58′ 14.915″ N   23° 43′ 36.580″ E

Founded in about 420 BC, the Sanctuary of Asklepios was dedicated to Asclepius, the god of medicine. It was a healing center and contained a temple and altar. Votive offerings, many which depict body parts, have been discovered at the site.

Theatre of Dionysus —

37.9703306, 23.7278099 / 37° 58′ 13.190″ N   23° 43′ 40.116″ E

Located at the eastern end of the south slope is the Theatre of Dionysus. It was constructed in the late 6th century BC. When it was later expanded in the 4th century BC, reports estimate it could seat anywhere from 17,000 to 25,000.

Other historical scenes are located along the south slope of the Acropolis. These include the **Stoa of Eumenes II** which runs eastward from the Odeon of Herodes Atticus, a **Byzantine Cistern**, the **Temple of Themis**, the **Choragic Monument of Nikias**, the **Sanctuary of Dionysus**, and the small **Chapel of Saint George Alexandrinos**.

Mars Hill / The Areopagus —

37.9722616, 23.7233694 / 37° 58′ 20.142″ N   23° 43′ 24.130″ E

Perhaps the most important site in Christian history in Athens is Mars Hill. It is located about 300 feet northwest of the Acropolis. Areopagus means Hill of Ares.

This rocky outcropping is no match in style to the grandeur of the temples which surrounded it, but for generations it was where the Areopagus Council met. It was to this site that some of the Epicurean and Stoic philosophers took Paul to hear about what he was teaching.

...but we follow him on up the gentle slope and watch him climb the stone steps, till at last he takes his stand on the top of that celebrated rock, where religious questions were wont to be discussed and settled in the presence of the assembled wisdom of Athens. We pause as he stands erect, with confident air, in the presence of sages and philosophers. But we are not kept long in suspense, for the hero of the Christian age begins his labors at once. He does not introduce his speech with flattery or apology. His cause is just, and he begins by assailing their own practices by saying, "Ye men of Athens, in all things I perceive ye are too superstitious," sending a dangerous dagger into the heart of their teachings and doctrines, and then begins one of the greatest sermons recorded in any book.

— ANDY T. RITCHIE
TRAVELS IN BIBLE LANDS
NASHVILLE: MCQUIDDY PRINTING COMPANY, 1922

Paul then preached what is probably his best-known sermon. Some who heard the sermon believed. Among them was Dionysius the Areopagite. This description would suggest he was a member of the Areopagus Council.

North of Areopagus/Mars Hill —

Athens State Prison Remains —

37.9737888, 23.7211471 / 37° 58′ 25.640″ N 23° 43′ 16.130″ E

This prison was built in 450 BC and is just south of the agora. It was the prison which housed Socrates. He was tried and sentenced to death by the drinking of hemlock. Friends visited him on his last day in prison. He drank the hemlock and died in 399 BC. There is a difference of opinion as to whether Socrates died in this prison or in the "Prison of Socrates" which is about 1,500 feet south of the Athens State Prison.

The difficulty, my friends, is not in avoiding death, but in avoiding unrighteousness; for that runs faster than death.

— Socrates, 399 BC

Hadrian's Aqueduct —

37.9739480, 23.7242163 / 37° 58′ 26.213″ N 23° 43′ 27.179″ E

Roman Emperor Hadrian commissioned this aqueduct in 125, and it was completed about 140. Water flowed from Mount Parnitha which is about 15 miles north of Athens, and it provided water to the city of Athens by infiltrating the groundwater.

Over the centuries it fell into disrepair. In 2018, the Athens Water Supply and Sewerage Company began exploring ways to rehabilitate the system so it would once again supply water to Athens.

Ancient Agora of Athens —

37.9748813, 23.7220834 / 37° 58′ 29.573″ N 23° 43′ 19.500″ E

Also known as the Classical Agora, the Ancient Agora of Athens was the heart of the city — it was the "town square." There you would find the commercial, political, social, religious, and administrative centers. The American School of Classical Studies at Athens has been excavating the Agora since 1931.

Middle Stoa of the Ancient Agora

37.9745888, 23.7232296 / 37° 58′ 28.520″ N 23° 43′ 23.627″ E

The Middle Stoa created a north and south area of the agora. It was built around 175 BC. It was a Doric style with the center colonnade having 23 columns. The ruins give an excellent perspective of its relationship to the Agora.

Odeon of Agrippa

37.9750466, 23.7231419 / 37° 58′ 30.168″ N   23° 43′ 23.311″ E

In 15 BC, Roman statesman and general Marcus Vipsanius Agrippa built this two-story odeon which could seat 1,000 people. It was destroyed in 267. The remains of two large statues of the Giants and Tritons which were set on high pedestals can be see today.

The Museum of the Ancient Agora in the Stoa of Attalos is a nice small museum. One of the displays contains fragments of a monument base with an inscription celebrating the Athenians victories over the Persians 490–480 BC. It was in 490 BC when the Athenians gained a decisive victory over the Persians in the Battle of Marathon.

Stoa of Attalos / Museum of the Ancient Agora

37.9752651, 23.7240516 / 37° 58′ 30.954″ N   23° 43′ 26.586″ E

Immediately east of the Odeon of Agrippa is the Stoa of Attalos and Museum of the Ancient Agora.

Construction of the Stoa began in 159 BC and was completed in 138 BC. It was built by King Attalos II of Pergamon and was given to the city of Athens in appreciation for the education he received in Athens. It was a two story design and believed to have had 21 shops on each level.

In the 1950s, the American School of Classical Studies reconstructed the Stoa on its original foundation. This project was funded by the Rockefeller family.

It now houses the Museum of the Ancient Agora and is home to many items discovered during the excavation of the Agora.

Monument of Socrates and Confucius

37.9743882, 23.7232925 / 37° 58′ 27.798″ N   23° 43′ 23.853″ E

This monument was unveiled in 2021 and celebrates the diplomatic ties between Greece and China which marked its 50th anniversary in 2022.

Immediately East of the
Monument of Socrates and Confucius

Library of Pantainos

37.9744447, 23.7244954 / 37° 58′ 28.001″ N   23° 43′ 28.183″ E

The library was built late in the 1st century AD by Athenian philosopher Titus Flavius Pantainos. Archaeologists discovered a white marble plaque which gave the rules of the library: "No book shall be taken out, since we have sworn it. It will be open from the first hour until the sixth."

Roman Forum

37.9742519, 23.7260787 / 37° 58′ 27.307″ N   23° 43′ 33.883″ E

In 51 BC, Julius Caesar pledged to build a forum in Athens. Later, Augustus donated the funds and the Roman Forum was constructed late 1st century BC.

Horologion of Andronikos Kyrrhestes

37.9741859, 23.7270199 / 37° 58′ 27.069″ N   23° 43′ 37.272″ E

Within the Roman Forum is the Horologion of Andronikos Kyrrhestes, also known as the Tower of the Winds. It is an octagonal building and construction was completed about 50 BC. It incorporated sundials, a water clock, and a wind vane. Each of the eight sides has a relief which depicts the characteristic of the wind from that direction.

Monument of the Eponymous Heroes

37.9750964, 23.7223820 / 37° 58′ 30.347″ N   23° 43′ 20.575″ E

The earliest reference to this monument is 424 BC when Aristophanes wrote something about it. It was a marble base with 10 bronze statues representing the tribes of Athens. What remains today is a base for the 10 statues and a fence that is partially restored.

Altar of Zeus Agoraios

37.9751773, 23.7225225 / 37° 58' 30.638" N 23° 43' 21.081" E

During the excavations of 1931, the Altar of Zeus Agoraios was one of the first discoveries made. Originally dating to the 5th or 4th century BC, this altar was made of limestone and used in a variety of religious ceremonies. Its footprint is only about 30 feet by 15 feet.

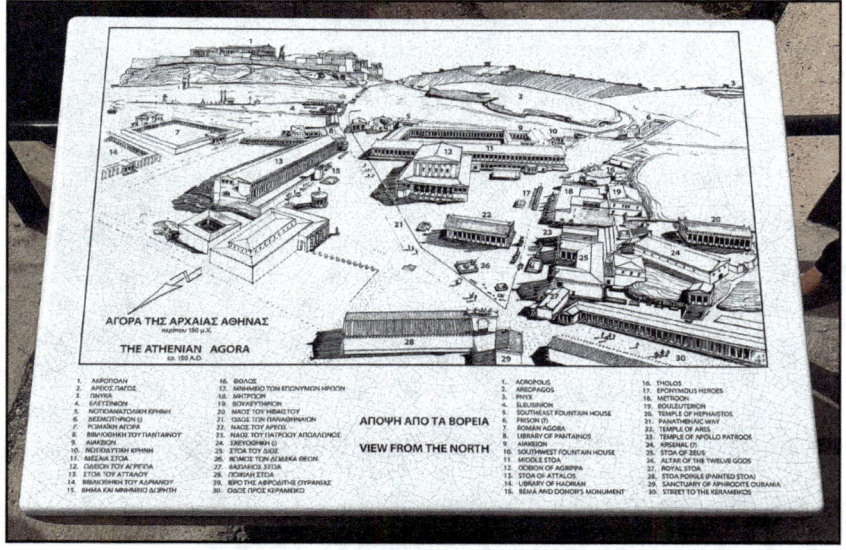

This is a photo of the site map looking from the north (bottom) to the south (top). Building #13 is the Stoa of Attalos, and building #20 is the Temple of Hephaestus. In the upper left you can see the Acropolis.

Temple of Ares

37.9755348, 23.7227535 / 37° 58' 31.925" N 23° 43' 21.913" E

Originally erected near Mount Hymettus about 430 BC, it was moved to the Agora in the early part of the 1st century AD. It was originally dedicated to Athena Pallenis. After being moved, it was dedicated to Ares. In the 5th century, Christians defaced the structure, and it was demolished in the 6th century.

Altar of the Twelve Gods —

37.9758028,23.7226561 / 37° 58' 32.890" N 23° 43' 21.562" E

Pisistratus the Younger set up the Altar of the Twelve Gods during his time in public office in 522-521 BC. It is possible that the altar was dedicated to the twelve gods on the east frieze of the Parthenon: Zeus, Hera, Poseidon, Demeter, Athena, Ares, Hephaestus, Dionysus, Apollo, Artemis, Hermes, and Aphrodite.

The altar became the point from which distances to Athens were measured. Very few remains of the altar are visible today as the Athens Metro runs through the area.

The photo above shows a few of the many ruins scattered around the Ancient Agora of Athens.

The beautifully designed capital of the Corinthian order on the left is from the Odeon of Agrippa.

Temple of Apollo Patroos

37.9755270, 23.7221251 / 37° 58′ 31.897″ N   23° 43′ 19.650″ E

There is little left to see of this small temple which was originally constructed about 535 BC. It was dedicated to Apollo who is considered to be the father of the Ionian race.

Temple of Hephaestus

37.9755816, 23.7214672 / 37° 58' 32.094" N   23° 43' 17.282" E

This well-preserved Temple of Hephaestus was completed in 415 BC to honor Hephaestus, the Greek god of metalworking, craftsmanship, sculpture, and fire. The temple, which is built with Pentelic marble, has Doric order columns — six on the east and west sides and thirteen on the north and south sides. There are numerous sculptures on the temple, and the west side depicts the fall of Troy.

Beginning around 700, it served as the Greek Orthodox Church of Saint George Akamates until 1834.

Our group makes its way to the Temple of Hephaestus on our visit in April 2024. — PHOTO BY CRAIG CHEATHAM

Sanctuary of Aphrodite Urania —

37.9759789, 23.7217192 / 37° 58' 33.524" N   23° 43' 18.189" E

Around 500 BC, a marble altar was built to honor Aphrodite Urania (of the heavens). The temple fell into ruin, but it became known because Pausanias, who was a 2nd century AD travel writer, mentioned it in his book, *Description of Greece*.

Statue of Theseus ——

37.9763492, 23.7211292 / 37° 58′ 34.857″ N   23° 43′ 16.065″ E

At the northernmost point of this section is an impressive statue of Theseus who is the mythical king and founder of Athens. Renowned sculptor George Vitalis created the statue in 1868.

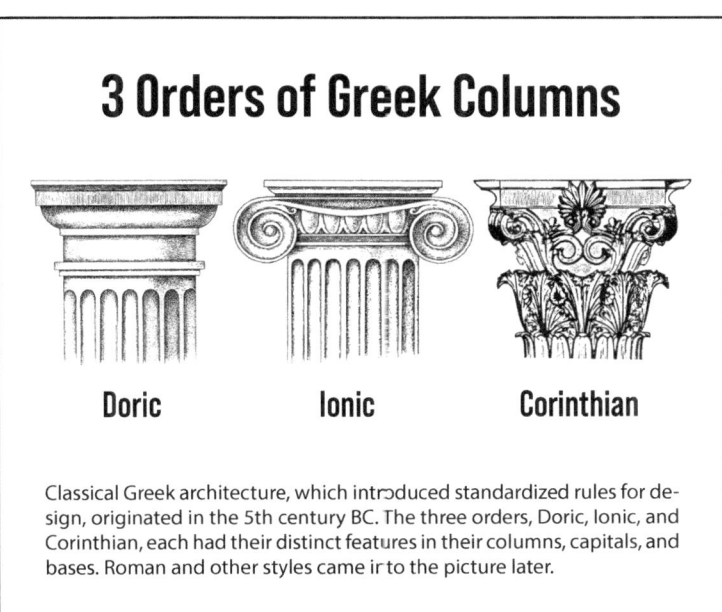

3 Orders of Greek Columns

Doric   Ionic   Corinthian

Classical Greek architecture, which introduced standardized rules for design, originated in the 5th century BC. The three orders, Doric, Ionic, and Corinthian, each had their distinct features in their columns, capitals, and bases. Roman and other styles came into the picture later.

Across the Tracks —

When the Athens and Piraeus Railway Company laid their tracks and began operating in 1869, a section of the line ran across the northern area that surrounded the Ancient Agora of Athens. The Athens Metro now runs along these rails.

Between the tracks and Adrianou Street (which is the oldest commercial street in Athens) are the **Royal Stoa (Stoa Basileios)** and a **Roman Basilica**.

The Royal Stoa was constructed about 525 BC with a style of the Doric order. Although it was not the largest stoa, it was the stoa where copies of the laws were kept and many legal matters handled.

Crossing Adrianou Street we have the **Stoa Poikile (Painted Porch)** which was built about 460 BC. It was built by Peisianax and originally known as the "Peisianactean Stoa."

The magnificent Philopappos Monument stands tall and is a reminder of those who helped make Athens a great city.

Southwest of the Acropolis —

Southwest of the Acropolis is a large green space of approximately 124 acres. There are a number of paths and trails in this area, and there are a couple of places that provide great vistas. From these areas there are many great views of the city of Athens, the Acropolis, and the Aegean Sea.

In this area are three hills: **Philopappos Hill** (also known as Hill of the Muses), **Hill of the Pnyx**, and **Hill of the Nymphs**. Although it does not have the ruins, temples, and monuments that other areas around the Acropolis have, there are a few sites to notice.

Philopappos Monument —

37.9673598, 23.7214369 / 37° 58' 2.495" N 23° 43' 17.173" E

This two story monument is built upon Philopappos Hill and was dedicated to Athenian citizen and Roman consul Gaius Julius Antiochus Epiphanes Philopappos. It was completed about 116.

Pnyx Monument —

37.9714559, 23.7192616 / 37° 58′ 17.241″ N   23° 43′ 9.342″ E

This small rocky hill may be the most important site in Athens in the history of the development of democracy. As early as 507 BC, following the reforms of ancient Athenian lawgiver Cleisthenes, citizens would gather here for political discussions.

Hill of the Nymphs —

37.9722283, 23.7181927 / 37° 58′ 20.022″ N   23° 43′ 5.494″ E

This hill received its name in 1835 when archaeologists discovered an inscriptions dedicating the area to nymphs. It is home to the National Observatory of Athens which is surrounded by beautiful gardens.

Also in this area is the **Prison of Socrates**, **Kimon's Tomb**, **Deaf Man's Cave**, **Seven Seats Plateau**, **Sanctuary of Pan**, and the remains of the **Heroon of Mousaios**.

The Temple of Olympian Zeus welcomes people to a beautiful green space filled with gardens.

Elsewhere in Athens —

Because of the abundance of archaeological ruins, monuments, and historical sites in Athens, time and space does not allow us to list all of these.

About 1,500 feet east of the Acropolis (as the crow flies) is a green area of about 115 acres with some interesting sites. This area is bounded by Highways 1, 91, and 54. One entrance to this area is the Arch of Hadrian.

Arch of Hadrian —

37.9701778, 23.7320205 / 37° 58′ 12.640″ N   23° 43′ 55.274″ E

In the southwest corner of this green space is the 59-foot-tall marble Arch of Hadrian. Erected about 131, the arch is believed to be a dividing line between ancient Athens and Hadrian's Athens. One side is inscribed "This is Athens, the ancient city of Theseus;" the other side has this inscription: "This is the city of Hadrian, and not of Theseus." The city of Hadrian was known as Hadrianopolis.

Evangelos Zappas had a desire for the Olympic Games to return to Greece and was a major influence on the Zappian Olympic Games which preceeded the modern Olympic Games.

Temple of Olympian Zeus —

37.9693790, 23.7330982 / 37° 58′ 9.764″ N   23° 43′ 59.154″ E

The grandeur of the Temple of Olympian Zeus can be seen in the few remaining columns topped with highly-detailed capitals of the Corinthian order. Construction of the temple began about 520 BC by Peisistratus. Later, the project came to a halt and was dormant for over 300 years. From 174-164 BC Seleucid King Antiochus IV Epiphanes worked on the project. Roman Emperior Hadrian ultimately finished the project and oversaw its dedication in 132 AD.

Zappeion Megaron —

37.9714726, 23.7366559 / 37° 58′ 17.301″ N   23° 44′ 11.961″ E

This large elegant building was constructed for the revival of the modern Olympic Games and opened on October 20, 1888. In front of it is the **Zappeion Garden**, a tree-filled park with walking paths, statues, and a beautiful fountain. The hall is now a conference center for both public and private purposes. Immediately north of the Zeppeion Hall is the **National Garden**. Within the National Garden are Roman ruins, **Queen Amalia's Pergola**, **National Garden Children's Library**, **Spanish Fountain**, and walking paths.

Tomb of the Unknown Soldier —
37.9753694, 23.7361948 / 37° 58′ 31.330″ N 23° 44′ 10.301″ E

Just northwest of the National Garden is the Tomb of the Unknown Soldier. Sculptor Fokion Rok fashioned the tomb between 1930 and 1932. It honors Greek soldiers who have died fighting for the nation. Framing the tomb are steps which have the names of the various wars engraved in them. The tomb is guarded by the Evzones — the Greek Presidential Guard — who are an elite group of soldiers.

Hellenic Parliament Building —
37.9753260, 23.7369092 / 37° 58′ 31.174″ N 23° 44′ 12.873″ E

Immediately east of the Tomb of the Unknown Soldier is the Greek Parliament House.

Syntagma Square —
37.9755434, 23.7348770 / 37° 58′ 31.956″ N 23° 44′ 5.557″ E

Syntagma Square, or Constitution Square, is across Leof Vasilissis Olgas (Highway 91) to the west of the Tomb of the Unknown Soldier. On September 3, 1843, the people of Athens gathered in Syntagma Square, rebelled against King Otto, and demanded a constitution.

Panathenaic Stadium —
37.9693050, 23.7402641 / 37° 58′ 9.498″ N 23° 44′ 24.951″ E

Originally constructed in the 4th century BC, the Panathenaic Stadium went through several changes over the centuries. In about 144, Roman Senator Herodes Atticus rebuilt the stadium completely with marble. In 1869, it was excavated, and in 1870 and 1875 hosted the Zappas Olympics. In 1896, it was the site for the opening and closing ceremonies for the first modern Olympics. In 2004, it was used as a venue for the XXVIII Olympic Games.

*Athen's Panathenaic Stadium is an impressive structure. It
is built entirely of marble and can seat 45,000 people.*

Hadrian's Library —

37.9755155, 23.7259716 / 37° 58′ 31.856″ N   23° 43′ 33.498″ E

In about 132, Roman Emperor Hadrian established a library in Athens. Its inner courtyard was about 367 feet by 269 feet and showcased 100 columns. Not only was it a repository for important literary
works and legal documents, it was a place which hosted lectures.

The Plaka —

Nestled against the northern and eastern slopes of the Acropolis is
the oldest — and most famous — neighborhood in Athens, the Plaka.
Because of being next to the Acropolis, it is known as the "Neighborhood of the Gods." This picturesque neighborhood offers places to
stay, eat, and shop. It is home to the Metropolitan Cathedral of Athens
which was dedicated on May 21, 1862.

Lycabettus Hill —

37.9818761, 23.7431314 / 37° 58′ 54.754″ N   23° 44′ 35.273″ E

Lycabettus Hill is the highest point in Athens reaching 908 feet above
sea level. You can take the Lycabettus Funicular to the top, but most
of the trip is in a tunnel. On the summit, you can enjoy a great meal,
have a wonderful view of the surrounding area, and visit the whitewashed 18th Church of St. George.

National Archaeological Museum

37.9891596, 23.7318151 / 37° 59 20.975" N   23° 43' 54.534" E

Established in 1829, the National Archaeological Museum has been in its present location since 1889. The neoclassical designed structure is the largest museum in Greece. It covers over 86,000 square feet and houses five major permanent collections: the Collection of Prehistoric Antiquities, the Sculpture Collection, the Vase and Minerals Collection, the Metallurgical Works Collection, and the Greece Collection of Egyptian and Eastern Antiquities, some of which date back to 5000 BC.

Items in the museum include the gold funeral mask of Agamemnon from about 1550–1500 BC, gold elliptical funeral diadems, gold Mycenean cups, statue of Asklepius, bronze statue of Zeus or Poseidon, bronze pitchers, frescoes, Egyptian necklaces, the oldest attic epigraphy dating from the 8th century BC, and the main fragment from the Antikythera mechanism from the 2nd century BC. The Antikythera mechanism was the inspiration for the Archimedes Dial in *Indiana Jones and the Dial of Destiny*.

The museum has a 118-year-old archaeological library containing some 20,000 volumes.

Currently, a 220,000 square foot underground extension is being built. It is to be completed by 2028 and will feature a rooftop garden.

Reflections ...

Because Paul was preaching Jesus and the resurrection, the religious leaders and philosophers of Athens were confused. The name of Jesus was not familiar to them; they didn't have a temple to Him; the teaching was different from anything they had ever heard.

As Paul spoke to them, he began with where they were and what they believed. He stated, "Men of Athens, I perceive that in every way you are very religious" (Acts 17:22). He then commented on their altars including the one to the "unknown god."

Some people believe that Paul's statement about their being very religious was made in a cynical fashion. I don't share that view. I believe Paul was being very direct to them and addressing their practices.

He said, "There is one more, and I'm telling you about Him." He then moved to making statements about God which I'm sure caused them to wonder, think, and question.

Among the affirmations Paul made are these:

◆ "The God who made the world and everything in it, being Lord of heaven and earth, does not live in temples made by man" (Acts 17:24). This concept would be totally foreign to them.

◆ He told them that it is because of God that we "live and move and have our being" (Acts 17:28). Going from multiple deities to a single God would challenge their polytheistic thinking.

◆ He spoke about repentence, judgment, righteousness, and the resurrection of the dead. Repentence, judgment, and righteousness might have been palatable to them, but the idea of a resurrection from the dead was not acceptable and must be rejected.

In his discussions with the Athenians and in his sermon, Paul integrated faith and reason.

In our lives today, may we have a burning desire to let God rule in our lives and be completely accepting of His holiness, guidance, and principles because we have a risen Savior.

Chapter 20

Paul & the Panhellenic Games

Did you ever wonder what the apostle Paul's favorite sport may have been? Did he eagerly await the next sporting competition? Where did Paul get his knowledge of sports?

When the apostle Paul wrote the Christians at Corinth, he addressed the many issues they were having, but he later reemphasized the focus of his ministry: to win souls for Jesus Christ (1 Corinthians 9:13-23).

Because Corinth was the home of the Isthmian Games, he then used a sports metaphor that people would understand. "Do you not know that in a race all the runners run, but only one receives the prize? So run that you may obtain it. Every athlete exercises self-control in all things. They do it to receive a perishable wreath, but we an imperishable. So I do not run aimlessly; I do not box as one beating the air. But I discipline my body and keep it under control, lest after preaching to others I myself should be disqualified" (1 Corinthians 9:24-27).

Paul used sports imagery many times in his epistles.

There were four games that were popular for centuries.

Olympic Games at Olympia —

The most famous games are the Olympic Games. The earliest recorded games were in 776 BC at Olympia in honor of Zeus. In those games Coroebus of Elis won a footrace and became the first Olympic champion. Games were held every four years, and other events were introduced as the years passed.

Greece came under Roman rule during the 2nd century BC. Because the Romans looked on the athletic events with contempt, the Olympic Games were eventually abandoned in 394.

The Olympic Games were revitalized in 1896 because of the dream of Pierre de Coubertin. He originally wanted his home of Paris, France, to host the Games in 1900. However, 34 nations urged him to begin the Games in 1896 in Athens, Greece.

The important thing in life is not the triumph but the struggle, the essential thing is not to have conquered but to have fought well.

— Pierre de Coubertin, father of the modern Olympic Games

In today's Olympic Games, the torch is lit in Olympia, Greece, and a relay begins with the run concluding in the host city.

Isthmian Games at Corinth —

The Isthmian Games were held at the Isthmus of Corinth to honor Poseidon who ruled the seas. The games began in 582 BC and were held every two years in April or May. In addition to athletic events, the Isthmian Games also included music and poetry competitions. These games continued into the 4th century AD.

Nemean Games at Nemea —

Although there are some myths surrounding how the Nemean Games came to be, they probably started in 573 BC. They were held every two years in July to honor Zeus. These games were for Greek-born men, and some records state they were only open to soldiers. The competition included both athletic and equestrian events.

In 271 BC, the Nemean Games were moved to Argos where they continued for a period of time.

Initial archaeological excavations began in 1884 by French archaeologists. In 1924-26 and again in 1964, the American School of Classical Studies in Athens pursued more comprehensive excavations.

In 1973, the University of California, Berkeley, undertook excavations at Nemea with Professor Stephen G. Miller (June 22, 1942 – August 11, 2021) directing the work. On July 19, 1974, Miller and his team discovered the starting line of the ancient track about 22 feet below the modern surface. UC Berkeley continues to manage the site and the museum.

In 1994, the Nemean Games were revived. In their Statement of Purpose, The Society for the Revival of the Nemean Games said, "It is our belief that the modern Olympic Games, despite their obvious success in many respects, have become increasingly removed from the average person. Our goal is the participation, on the sacred ancient earth of Greece, of anyone and everyone, in games that will revive the spirit of the Olympics. We will achieve this by reliving authentic ancient athletic customs in the ancient stadium of Nemea."

The 2024 games were held June 28-30.

Pictured is the ancient stadion at Nemea. Stadion can refer to 1) a unit of measurement equal to a little over 600 feet, 2) an ancient running event, or 3) the stadium in which the running event took place.
— PHOTO BY ROBIN IVERSEN RÖNNLUND / WIKIMEDIA

Archaelogical Site of Nemea
Temple of Zeus
37.8095311, 22.7104076 / 37° 48′ 34.312″ N   22° 42′ 37.467″ E

Archaeological Museum of Nemea
37.8076237, 22.7112468 / 37° 43′ 27.445″ N   22° 42′ 40.488″ E

Ancient Stadium of Nemea
37.8067390, 22.7145091 / 37° 48′ 24.260″ N   22° 42′ 52.233″ E

Pythian Games at Delphi —

The Pythian Games began about 582 BC in Delphi to honor Apollo. They were second in importance to the Olympics. In addition to various athletic events, they also included drama, music, poetry, and painting. The games were held in August every four years, and the last games were in 393 AD.

The Charioteer of Delphi which was discovered in 1896 stands in the Delphi Archaeological Museum.

On March 21, 1436, Delphi was rediscovered by Cyriacus of Ancona, an Italian classical scholar. It was centuries later — in the second half of the 19th century — when archaeological investigations began to take place. In 1892, Théophile Homolle and the French Archaeological School of Athens began a systematic excavation. Finds included the Stadium and the Theatre. One of the most exceptional discoveries was the Charioteer of Delphi which was discovered in 1896. The excavations lasted 10 years and led to the creation of the Delphi Archaeological Museum.

Heraean Games

Because the Olympic Games were initially just for men, the Heraean Games were established for young girls and were believed to be a rite of passage into adulthood. These games began at some point after 776 BC — perhaps as late as 580 BC — to honor the Greek goddess Hera. They were held every four years at the Olympic stadium in Olympia although at a different time than the Olympic Games.

The games consisted of a footrace, and the winner received a crown of olive leaves. The games were discontinued in 393 AD.

Chapter 21

Temple of Poseidon – By the Sea

37.6501805, 24.0245737 / 37° 39′ 0.650″ N 24° 1′ 28.465″ E

Offering a stunning view because of being located at Cape Sounion on the tip of the Attiki Peninsula, the Temple of Poseidon dates from the 5th century BC.

Sitting at an elevation of 200 and overlooking the sea, sailors could see the Temple of Poseidon from quite a distance.

— PHOTO BY DAVID IGLESIAS / PEXELS

This Doric-style temple is made entirely of white marble and was dedicated to Poseidon who, in Greek mythology, ruled over seas, water, storms, earthquakes, and horses. He is often pictured holding a trident, and his Roman name is Neptune.

It is only natural that this temple would be built where departing, arriving, and passing ships would have an excellent view of a structure dedicated to the one who ruled over the seas and thus, was the one who provided a safe passage for them.

Because of being located over an hour south of Athens and off the beaten path, many tour groups do not include this temple on their itinerary.

The restoration and reconstruction of the Temple of Poseidon shows its stately columns.

— PHOTO BY RANYA / PIXABAY

Archaeology in Sounion —

Valerios Stais oversaw excavations of both the Temple of Poseidon and the Temple of Athena between 1897 and 1915. He and his team uncovered pottery, scarabs, seals, sculptures, amulets, and other items.

The excavations led to the reconstruction of the Temple of Poseidon as it is seen today. However, only a few items help define the footprint of the Temple of Athena which is just a short distance from the Temple of Poseidon.

Over the years, many people have carved their names in the remains of the temple — and thus desecrated it. Perhaps the most notable inscription is the one supposedly made by Lord Byron.

Lord Byron traveled to Greece in 1810-1811. He later returned to fight the Ottoman Empire in Greek's War of Independence. He died in battle April 19, 1824.

His love for Greece was undisputed. One piece he wrote was "The Isles of Greece." Toward the end of this 96-line poem he paid tribute to Sounior with these words:

> *Place me on Sunium's marbled steep,*
> *Where nothing, save the waves and I,*
> *May hear our mutual murmurs sweep;*
> *There, swan-like, let me sing and die...*

This photo, which was taken from Acrocorinth, shows the Gulf of Corinth on the left with the Saronic Gulf visible in the right half of the photo. The Corinth Canal made it possible for ships to transit from one gulf to the other.

— PHOTO BY DALE W. MANOR

Chapter 22
Corinth Canal – Crossing the Isthmus

The Corinth Canal is a popular attraction because of its being an engineering marvel and because of people who love to bungee jump off of a perfectly good bridge.

The canal creates a passageway across the isthmus between the Saronic Gulf and the Gulf of Corinth.

The depth of the Corinth Canal is impressive as you view the length of the canal.

However, the canal has not always been there. During the Cypselid Dynasty of ancient Corinth, Periander (627-587 BC) was the second ruler. He brought prosperity to the area but was believed by many to be a harsh and cruel ruler. He understood the immense sea dangers for ships sailing around the Peloponnesian Peninsula so he proposed building a canal across the isthmus. However, he was stymied by the massiveness of the project, and he also received an oracle from Delphi counseling him against building a canal.

Although Periander did not build the canal, he did construct the Diolkos. This paved trackway allowed ships or their merchandise to be moved across the isthmus on wheeled carts.

Other leaders kicked around the idea of building a canal, but it was Nero who took a golden pickaxe to the project in 67 AD. Some progress was made, but Nero died the next year, and the project was abandoned. There is a weather-worn relief of Nero near the northwest end of the canal.

In the 17th century, others tried to construct a canal but were unsuccessful.

— Corinth Bridge —
37.9270912, 22.9945800 / 37° 55′ 37.528″ N   22° 59′ 40.488″ E

— Relief of Nero —
37.9452680, 22.9687611 / 37° 56′ 42.965″ N   22° 58′ 7.540″ E

— Diolkos —
37.9492705, 22.9625177 / 37° 56′ 57.374″ N   22° 57′ 45.064″ E

Work began once more on the canal in 1882. The invention of dynamite in 1867 by Alfred Nobel allowed for the blasting of stone. Hungarian engineers Istvan Türr and Bela Gerster guided the work, and hundreds of workmen toiled to see its completion in 1893.

The canal is an engineering marvel about 4 miles long. The channel is 26 feet deep. The rock walls rise about 300 feet and are separated by 81 feet at the top and 70 feet at the bottom.

In addition to being a transit way for pleasure craft, tourist boats, and commercial ships sailing between the gulfs, the canal has become a popular spot for bungee jumping. Jumps are made from the Corinth Bridge at the canal.

In recent years, the canal had a couple of landslides, but reconstruction has taken place and ships are again sailing between the Gulf of Corinth and the Saronic Gulf.

In the Archaeological Museum of Ancient Corinth is this stone inscription which is a poem in Latin telling about Marc Antony's grandfather transporting the Roman fleet across the Isthmus in 102 BC.

We visited the remnants of the ancient Diolkos at the north end of the Corinth Canal. You can see the blue water of the canal toward the top of the photo where some of our group are standing.

Chapter 23

Corinth – Saints by Calling

37.9061395, 22.8780213 / 37° 54′ 22.102″ N   22° 52′ 40.877″ E

Ancient Corinth is on the Peloponnesian Peninsula and about 50 miles west of Athens. The area shows signs of having been occupied as early as 3,000 – 4,000 BC — perhaps earlier.

As one entered Corinth via the Lechaion Road they would pass by bath houses, a basilica, court yards, and businesses. At the end of the road is the bema, the judgment seat of Corinth. Looking past the end of the road, Acrocorinth rises in the distance.

In the early 8th century BC, the city-state of Corinth began to establish a vibrant commercial center. Having gained control of the isthmus aided its development. Over the next couple of centuries the area was ruled by the Bacchaid family. However, they were later over-thrown by Cypselus. He, along with his son Periander who followed him, were tyrants.

One of Periander's positive accomplishments was the construction of the Diolkos, a paved trackway which aided in the transportation of ships and goods across the isthmus.

About 550 BC, an oligarchical government was established. The City of Athens was its commercial rival, and that created political rivalry. In the Peloponnesian War (431-404 BC) Corinth joined with Sparta to fight against Athens.

In 400 BC, Corinth had a population of about 90,000. Corinth's independence ended in 338 BC when Philip II of Macedon brought his troops in, took control of the region, and established the League of Corinth.

The city was destroyed by Rome in 146 BC, and a new Corinth was built in 44 BC upon the orders of Julius Caesar.

Paul in Corinth —

Paul arrived in Corinth after traveling across Macedonia and spending some time in Athens. Acts 18:1-18 relates the story of Paul's time in Corinth. Some things to note about his stay in Corinth:

  1) Paul met Aquila and Priscilla.

  2) Every Sabbath he reasoned in the synagogue.

  3) Many believed — including the synagogue leader — and were baptized into Jesus Christ.

  4) Paul stayed there a year and a half.

  5) Gallio was proconsul and came to Paul's defense.

On Paul's third missionary journey, we see that he stayed in Greece for three months (Acts 20:2-3). This is probably a reference to Corinth. Paul's words in 2 Corinthians 2:1; 12:14; and 13:1 point to the possibility of a second visit and maybe a third visit to Corinth.

Paul's Letters to the Corinthians —

In most English Bibles we have two letters from the apostle Paul to the Christians at Corinth, yet it is believed that he may have written four letters. In 1 Corinthians 5:9, he references a previous letter. This make our 1 Corinthians the second letter he wrote.

In 2 Corinthians 2:4 and 7:8-9, Paul speaks about a letter which caused them grief. Some believe this is a reference to what we know as 1 Corinthians; others believe it is a letter written between the two we know as 1 & 2 Corinthians.

Some believe the letter we know as 2 Corinthians is a combined two letters with chapters 1-9 being one letter and chapters 10-13 being another letter. One of the reasons for this is the last few verses in chapter 9 sounding like a benediction/conclusion and the first few verses in chapter 10 sounding like an introduction/greeting.

These ruins which are close to the Peirene Fountain are just a few of the many ruins and artifacts which have been discovered in Corinth. The Archaeological Museum of Ancient Corinth has many items to see.

Archaeology in Corinth —

The American School of Classical Studies at Athens was founded in 1881 and has been excavating in ancient Corinth since 1896. They have centered their work around the section in which the 6th century BC Temple of Apollo is located.

As one approaches Corinth, the Temple of Apollo dominates the landscape. There are several other discoveries that offer insight into the daily life of the Corinthians and help enhance biblical understanding.

In 1932, the American School of Classical Studies built the Archaeological Museum of Ancient Corinth. The museum showcases many discoveries from the excavations.

Corinth

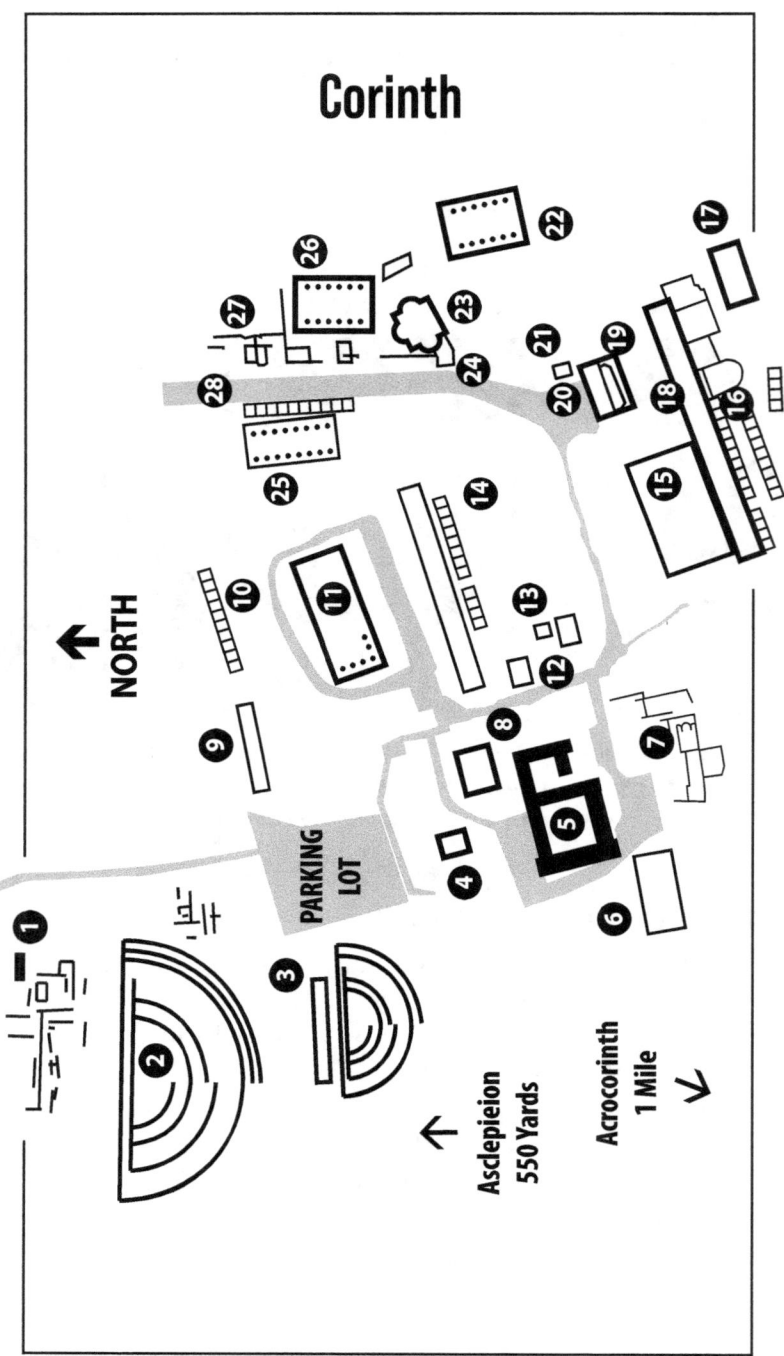

The Erastus Inscripton (above) states, "Erastus in return for his aedileship laid [the pavement] at his own expense." When Paul wrote the Roman Christians from Corinth, Erastus sent his greetings.

The few remaining columns from the Temple of Apollo stand out against the blue sky.

Sites for Corinth Map

1. Erastus Inscripton
2. Theatre
3. Odeon
4. Glauke Fountain
5. Archaeological Museum of Ancient Corinth
6. Temple E / Temple of Octavia
7. West Shops
8. Temple C
9. North Stoa
10. North Market
11. Temple of Apollo
12. West Terrace Temples
13. Babbius Monument
14. Sacred Spring

15. Sanctuary of Dionysus
16. Bouleuterion
17. South Basilica
18. South Stoa
19. Bema
20. Prisoner/Witness Column (?)
21. Heroon of the Crossroads
22. Julian Basilica
23. Peirene Fountain
24. Propylaia
25. Lechaion Road Basilica
26. Peribolos of Apollo
27. Eurycleus Baths
28. Lechaion Road

Sites To See —

Erastus Inscription —

37.9071398, 22.8775832 / 37° 54' 25.703" N   22° 52' 39.300" E

In 1929, excavations at Corinth unearthed a section of pavement with the following inscription, "Erastus in return for his aedileship laid (the pavement) at his own expense." This was during a period in which citizens built specific projects in the city because of the government not having the funds. The inscription is near the ancient theatre.

When Paul wrote the Christians at Rome from Corinth, he sent greetings from a number of people, including Erastus, the city treasurer (Romans 16:23).

It appears that Erastus joined Paul in his travels and was in Ephesus with him before being sent to Macedonia (Acts 19:22). When Paul wrote Timothy, he mentioned Erastus (2 Timothy 4:20).

Glauke Fountain —

37.9055561, 22.8781801 / 37° 54' 20.002" N   22° 52' 41.448" E

The Glauke Fountain was formed from the ridge of limestone on which the Temple of Apollo sits. It is a large cube with four large reservoirs and was constructed about the same time as the Temple of Apollo. It is believed that the fountain is named for the daughter of Creon, the mythological King of Corinth.

The Glauke Fountain sits close to the Archaeological Museum of Ancient Corinth. In the distance are the remaining pillars of the Temple of Apollo.

Archaeological Museum of Ancient Corinth —
37.9053309, 22.8783408 / 37° 54′ 19.191″ N 22° 52′ 42.027″ E

This fine museum was completed in 1932 and gives an excellent perspective on ancient Corinth. As you walk through the rooms, you move from the Prehistoric period through the various time periods to the Byzantine era. There are many rare and unique items.

One of the most interesting rooms contains findings from the Sanctuary of Asclepius. It is filled with ceramic body parts that were offered in thanks for healings.

In addition to various body parts discovered in the Sanctuary of Asclepios, the Archaeological Museum of Ancient Corinth contains many artifacts. To the right are various types of bowls.

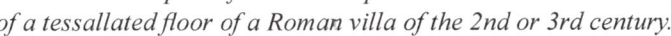

The museum holds a number of statues. The upper left photo shows the very detailed work by the sculptor.

To the right of the statue is a mosaic picturing Dionysos. It was part of the central panel of a tessallated floor of a Roman villa of the 2nd or 3rd century.

In the lower left is a sculpture of the Emperior Nero.

The item on the lower right is a Sigma Table. Although not much is known about these tables, some believe these were used by the early church in the agape meal. Whether that idea references the communion or a common meal is not known.

Temple of Apollo —

37.9059518, 22.8790790 / 37° 54' 21.426" N 22° 52' 44.684" E

As you approach Corinth, you see the remains of the Temple of Apollo. Seven stately well-preserved columns from this Doric order temple stand on a small rise where the temple once stood. The temple dates back to the 4th century BC and was dedicated to Apollo, the god of light and music. Each column was carved from a single block of stone rather than using multiple drums to create the column.

The remains of the Temple of Apollo capture your attention as you arrive in Ancient Corinth.

Market Place —

The large agora was the center of the town's activities — business, political, and social.

Bema of St Paul —

37.9051347, 22.8802609 / 37° 54' 18.485" N 22° 52' 48.939" E

"But when Gallio was proconsul of Achaia, the Jews made a united attack on Paul and brought him before the tribunal" (Acts 18:12)

This large elevated rostrum is where city official held trials and public meetings. It is the place of judgment and is where the apostle Paul stood trial before Gallio because of his teaching the gospel of Jesus

Christ. In front of the bema is a column about 30" tall which is believed to be where the witness/prisoner stood.

The bema, sometimes referred to as the Bema of St Paul because of its being where he stood before Gallio, was the judgment seat in Corinth.

In front of the bema was a post which some believe is where the witness or prisoner stood as they were testifying or as judgment was being passed. In the background is the agora and the remains of the Temple of Apollo.

As you start to leave the city by the Lechaion Road, you see the Peirene Fountain on the east side. It must have been a marvelous site when in its prime.

Peirene Fountain —

37.9057275, 22.8805601 / 37° 54' 20.619" N   22° 52' 50.016" E

This well-preserved ancient spring was a vital water source for the city of Corinth. One can still envision the beauty it once had. There are a couple of myths about the origin of the fountain: 1) Pegasus, the winged horse, struck the ground with his hoof and water gushed from from the spring, and 2) Peirene, who was a nymph, cried when her son was unintentionally killed by Artemis, and her tears turned into this fountain.

Lechaion Road —

The Lechaion Road leads into town from the Port of Corinth. It passes the Peirene Fountain and concludes at the agora. Paul probably walked this road when he entered Corinth.

Other areas of Corinth —

While in Corinth, you will also see the **Theatre of Ancient Corinth**, the **Odeon**, the **Sanctuary of Dionysos**, basilicas, and building and housing ruins along the Lechaion Road.

Reflections ...

As we read Paul's first letter to the Christians at Corinth, we see a church with a truckload of problems. Yet, Paul addressed them as saints, stated they were sanctified, invoked the blessings of God upon them, and gave thanks for them. Why? Because God gave us a ministry of reconciliation and not of division.

Their being saints did not absolve them in any way of sin that was rampant within the church and among various people. He addressed the problems individually and taught what type of correction needed to take place.

It was when Paul was in Corinth that he wrote the Christians at Rome asking, "What shall we say then? Are we to continue in sin that grace may abound?" His answer was, " By no means!" (Romans 6:1-2). His experience with the Corinthians may have been the inspiration for this question.

Among the things we learn from Paul's letters to these Christians are:

◆ Even with all their problems, Paul addressed them as saints.

◆ We are called to be ministers of reconciliation, not division.

◆ The solution to sin is being obedient to God's holy will.

Temple of Asklepios

37.9106901, 22.8775398 / 37° 54' 38.484" N 22° 52' 39.143" E

The Temple of Asklepios is located about 1,800 feet north of ancient Corinth. People would go there to be healed of various diseases and ailments. After being healed, people would leave votive offerings in appreciation of their being healed. These offerings would many times be terra cotta images of the body part that was healed.

In their excavations, archaeologists have discovered many of these offerings. Numerous examples are displayed in a room in the Archaeological Museum of Ancient Corinth.

> When the apostle Paul wrote the Christians at Corinth about their false sense of superiority and lack of unity, he appealed to their awareness of the body parts and wrote, "For the body does not consist of one member but of many. If the foot should say, 'Because I am not a hand, I do not belong to the body,' that would not make it any less a part of the body. And if the ear should say, 'Because I am not an eye, I do not belong to the body,' that would not make it any less a part of the body. If the whole body were an eye, where would be the sense of hearing? If the whole body were an ear, where would be the sense of smell? But as it is, God arranged the members in the body, each one of them, as he chose. If all were a single member, where would the body be? As it is, there are many parts, yet one body" (1 Corinthians 12:14-20).

Asklepios was a physician who was deified by the Greeks because of his knowledge of medicine. The original Hippocratic Oath began, "I swear by Apollo Healer, by Asclepius, by Hygieia, by Panacea, and by all the gods and goddesses, making them my witnesses…"

The Rod of Asklepios which illustrates a single serpant coiled around a staff is used by many medical organizations around the world as an element of their logo.

Acrocorinth
37.8908614, 22.8701547 / 37° 53' 27.101" N 22° 52' 12.557" E

With a height of almost 1,900 feet, Acrocorinth is an imposing monolithic rock that overlooks ancient Corinth and the surrounding area. It is just about an 8-9 minute drive from ancient Corinth.

Besides being a great attraction for tourists today, it was a necessary military asset in years gone by. It enabled the military to monitor and protect the isthmus and encompassing area.

You can easily spend a couple of hours on Acrocorinth strolling around, checking out the ancient ruins, and enjoying panoramic views in every direction. As you ascend Acrocorinth, you don't reach a plateau such as the Acropolis of Athens. When you're within the city walls, there are two summits you will want to visit.

Prior to entering the first gate, you'll walk across the remains of the moat. There are three massive gates built during different periods of history. The city was fortified by three enormous stone walls which have arrow slits for archers and larger openings for canons. There are defensive towers around the site.

By the third gate are a post-Byzantine church and an Ottoman fountain. Just inside that gate you'll see an Ottoman fountain and bath, a mosque, and the Church of St. Demetrios. Nearby are another church and mosque.

To the south is the two-story Frankish tower perched on the western summit. It offers a great view paths on Acrocorinth and of the surrounding territory.

On the eastern summit are the foundation stones of the Temple of Aphrodite. Nearby are the ruins of an early Christian basilica and an Ottoman tomb.

About 1,000 feet south of the remains of the Temple of Aphrodite is Upper Peirene Fountain. There is a structure in which you can walk down the steps and see waters from the spring.

From the eastern summit you get a great bird's-eye view of the Gulf of Corinth and the Saronic Gulf.

Chapter 24

Cenchrea – Commending a Dear Sister

37.8823422, 22.9928051 / 37° 52′ 56.432″ N 22° 59′ 34.098″ E

About six or seven miles east of Corinth is the Port of Cenchrea. Although its origin is not known, there are indications it was active in the 5th century BC and that it remained active into the 7th century AD. Because of its deep natural harbor and proximity to Corinth, it was a logical port for trade and passengers.

Whether or not Paul spent time evangelizing in Cenchrea is unknown. The only reference we have to Paul's being there was after he concluded his stay in Corinth and before he sailed for Caesarea, he stopped in Cenchrea and had his hair cut off "because of a vow he had taken" (Acts 18:18, NIV). He then boarded a ship and made a brief stop at Ephesus before continuing to Caesarea.

We do know there was a church in Cenchrea because as Paul closed his letter to the Christians at Rome, he commended (or introduced) to them "our sister Phoebe, a servant of the church in Cenchreae" (Romans 16:1). Phoebe was one who had helped Paul and others as they ministered for the cause of Jesus Christ. It seems evident that she carried Paul's letter to the saints at Rome.

In writing the Christians at Corinth, Paul stated that the "household of Stephanas were the first converts in Achaia"(1 Corinthians 16:15). Achaia is a large area and Stephanas could have been from Cenchrea, Corinth, or some other city.

When Paul wrote 2 Corinthians, he addressed it to "the church of God that is at Corinth, with all the saints who aare in the whole of Achaia" (2 Corinthians 1:1). We do infer from this that Paul knew Christians across Achaia and was probably instrumental in the establishment of other churches besides Corinth — including the church in Cenchrea.

From 1962-1969, Robert Scranton led an archaeological team and partially excavated the ancient harbor. Other excavations began in

2002. Discoveries have included early Roman tombs, warehouses, complexes that may have been dedicated to Greek gods, mosaic pavements, and a Christian basilica.

If the weather is right, you can still see remains of the ancient port in the Saronic Gulf.

The contemporary village of Kechries, Greece, has a population of a little over 200.

Reflections ...

In just a few words, we learn a lot about Phoebe. Although she is only mentioned in the Bible one time, those few words tell us a lot:

◆ Her character was such that Paul was willing to commend her.

◆ She was a servant in the church.

◆ She helped and blessed Paul and others in many ways.

SUCCORER / PATRON

prostatis (προστάτις, 4368), a feminine form of prostatis, denotes "a protectress, patroness"; it is used metaphorically of Phoebe in Rom. 16:2. It is a word of dignity, evidently chosen instead of others which might have been used (see, e.g., under HELPER), and indicates the high esteem with which she was regarded, as one who had been a protectress of many. *Prostates* was the title of a citizen in Athens, who had the responsibility of seeing to the welfare of resident aliens who were without civic rights. Among the Jews it signified a wealthy patron of the community.

— *Vine's Expository Dictionary of New Testament Words*

Chapter 25

Kuşadası – The Port for Ephesus

37.8627850, 27.2554841 / 37° 51′ 46.026″ N 27° 15′ 19.743″ E

Kuşadası has seen many civilizations since its founding by the Leleges people in 3000 BC. In the 11th century BC, the area was settled by the Aeolians and then the Ionians in the 9th century BC. In the 6th century BC, it became a part of the Kingdom of Lydia. It was during this period that Kuşadası became an important port and trade center.

Kuşadası and the area came under the rule of the Roman Empire around 200 BC.

Kuşadası is the port where we dock as we visit Ephesus and Miletus.

As you enter the harbor at Kuşadası, Türkiye, the city name stands out on the hill. The statue at the top of the hill honors Mustafa Kemal Atatürk, founder of the Republic of Turkey.

The Library of Celsus is the iconic image that comes to many people's minds when Ephesus is mentioned. It was completed about 135 AD, so Paul would not have seen it. Paul did spend a couple of years teaching in the Hall of Tyrannus which many believed was located in this area.

To the right you see the triple arches of the Gate of Mazaeus and Mithridates.

— PHOTO BY KAY MILLS

Chapter 26

Ephesus – A Rich History

37.9358204, 27.3456108 / 37° 56' 8.953" N 27° 20' 44.199" E

Legend has it that Ephesus was founded in the 11th century BC by the Ionian prince Androclos. As he searched for a new Greek settlement, he inquired of the oracle of Delphi. The oracle stated a boar and fish would show him the location. Androclos was frying fish one day when one flopped out of the frying pan and into some bushes. A wild boar was in the bushes and was scared by the flopping fish. The boar ran out of the bushes, and Androclos killed it. Androclos remembered the oracle, built a new settlement, and called it Ephesus.

There are other legends and stories about the founding of Ephesus. However, its history can be traced back to about 1000 BC. In the 7th century BC, Ephesus came under the rulership of Lydian kings. Persians ruled the area beginning in 546 BC, and Alexander the Great conquered it in 334 BC. In 263 BC, Egyptians ruled the area, and in 129 BC Romans took control of the area.

Ephesus suffered extensive damage during an earthquake in the 7th century AD.

Paul in Ephesus —

The first record we have of Paul's visiting Ephesus is as he was concluding his second missionary journey. He had spent time in Corinth where he met Priscilla and Aquilla. They sailed with him to Ephesus where Paul made a brief visit.

In this brief visit in Ephesus, he did what he normally did in a new city: "He himself went into the synagogue and reasoned with the Jews" (Acts 18:19). They asked him to stay, but his goal was to continue to Antioch. He did promise to return if it was God's will.

Paul then sailed to Antioch leaving Priscilla and Aquila in Ephesus where they continued to teach. It was there they met Apollos. Apollos was a believer and "being fervent in spirit, he spoke and taught accurately the things concerning Jesus" (Acts 18:25). However, he only knew about the baptism of John. Priscilla and Aquila "explained to him the way of God more adequately" (Acts 18:26).

When Paul arrived in Ephesus on his third missionary journey, he met some disciples and asked them, "Did you receive the Holy Spirit when you believed?" (Acts 19:2). When they replied they did not know about the Holy Spirit, he asked them about their baptism. They were like Apollos; they only knew about John's baptism.

Paul spoke to them about the baptism of Jesus, and they were then "baptized in the name of the Lord Jesus" (Acts 19:5).

Paul returned to the synagogue at Ephesus and spoke there for three months. However this caused some dissension. He left the synagogue, took the disciples with him, and they had daily discussions in the lecture hall of Tyrannus for two years (Acts 19:8-10). Paul not only taught publically, but he also taught from house to house spending a total of three years in Ephesus (Acts 20:20, 31).

It was during this period that both Jews and Greeks throughout Asia heard the word of the Lord (Acts 19:10).

While in Ephesus, Paul faced ups and downs. People were healed. There was a conflict with the demon possessed. People who had practiced sorcery and were converted to Jesus burned their books. Demetrius, who made shrines to Artemis, caused an uprising during which the crowd met at the theatre. There — for two hours — they cried out, "Great is Artemis of the Ephesians!" (Acts 19:34). After the uprising, Paul left for Macedonia.

Paul met with Christians from Ephesus one more time, and that was in Miletus. After he boarded the ship at Assos to return to Caesarea and Jerusalem, he stopped at Miletus. There he prayed with the elders from Ephesus, wept with them, blessed them, and warned them saying, "Pay careful attention to yourselves and to all the flock, in which the Holy Spirit has made you overseers, to care for the church of God, which he obtained with his own blood. I know that after my departure fierce wolves will come in among you, not sparing the flock; and from among your own selves will arise men speaking twisted things, to draw away the disciples after them" (Acts 20:28-30). Paul would never see them again.

Other Biblical References —

When writing the Christians at Corinth, Paul referenced Ephesus in 1 Corinthians 15:32 and 16:8. He wrote this letter to the church at Corinth from Ephesus.

When Paul was in a jail cell in Rome, he wrote letters which are identified as the prison epistles. In addition to a letter to the church at Ephesus, he also wrote Philippians, Colossians, and Philemon.

When Paul wrote his coworker Timothy, he encouraged him to remain in Ephesus and continue teaching and maturing disciples. In a later letter to Timothy, he noted how well Onesiphorus served at Ephesus. Several paragraphs later, he stated that he had sent Tychicus to Ephesus.

In The Revelation, Jesus wrote the church at Ephesus (Revelation 2:1-7). He commended them in some areas but expressed His concern because "you have abandoned the love you had at first" (Revelation 2:4). He then told them, "Remember therefore from where you have fallen; repent, and do the works you did at first" (Revelation 2:5).

Archaeology in Ephesus —

In 1858, John Turtle Wood, an architect from England, was commissioned to design railway stations for the Smyrna and Aidin Railway in Turkey.

Five years later, Wood resigned his commission so he could search for the Temple of Artemis in Ephesus. He entered into an agreement with the British Museum which gave him a permit and provided a small allowance. On December 31, 1869, he discovered the Temple of Artemis.

From 1895-1913, Otto Benndorf and Carl Humann pursued further excavations. In 1898, Benndorf founded Austrian Archaeological Institute which has continuously conducted studies in Ephesus. In 1954, the Ephesus Museum began excavating in Ephesus. Since that time, many areas have been excavated and restored.

During the 2022 excavation season, a new area that included a few shops was discovered in Domitian Square next to the State Agora. One of the shops apparently contained Christian souvenirs for pilgrims. Items discovered in the area included ceramic vessels, oil lamps, spearheads, and gold coins. Sabine Ladstätter, Director of the

Austrian Archeology Institute (ÖAI) from 2009 to 2024 and Head of the Ephesus Ancient City Excavations, stated, "This is the most important discovery in Ephesus Ancient City since the Terrace Houses in Ephesus, which are now cult buildings of the ancient city of Ephesus, were found 50 years ago." (Ladstätter passed away June 3, 2024, after a lengthy illness.)

The archaeological excavations and reconstruction of Ephesus are some of the most extensive in the ancient world. Major artifacts are in Ephesus Museum in Selçuk, Ephesus Museum in Vienna, and the British Museum in London.

Archaeologists of Ephesus

John Turtle Wood
(1821-1890)

Sabine Ladstätter
(1968-2024)

Otto Bendorff
(1821-1890)

Carl Humann
(1839-1896)

Sites to See —

When Paul sailed to Ephesus, he probably would have entered the city by way of Harbor Street. However, many tour groups enter through the upper gate in the southeastern part of Ephesus because that allows you to walk downhill as you tour the city.

As we tour Ephesus, we see a marvelous restoration of an ancient city. Much of what has been excavated and restored was built after the time during which Paul visited and lived there. It is believed that he would have been in Ephesus in 52 AD as he was completing his second journey. That would place him in Ephesus about 53-54 AD on his third journey.

As we enter Ephesus from the upper gate, we proceed past a lot of history on ancient streets. The world of the Ephesians keeps opening up with each step we take.

Following are highlights of many of the sites we see on our tours.

The number in parenthesis after the site name denotes the location on the city map.

Although scholars differ on a lot of dates, an effort has been made to give reasonable construction dates so the reader may have an understanding of which structures were there when the apostle Paul ministered in Ephesus.

Baths of Varius (1) —

Constructed: 2nd century AD

About the 2nd century, Varius, a wealthy Roman, financed the building of these baths for the convenience of people who stopped in Ephesus while traveling. This allowed them to rest and freshen up. The baths served not only the travelers but also the locals. It may have been used as a place to visit, socialize, and discuss business.

The baths were heated by a hypocaust system. This system allowed warm air to flow through a space below the floors, thus heating the floors, the rooms, and the baths. There were three pools: frigidarium (cold water), tepidarium (warm water) and caldarium (hot water). It is believed the structure was originally three stories. Beautiful mosaics were added to the long corridor in the 5th century.

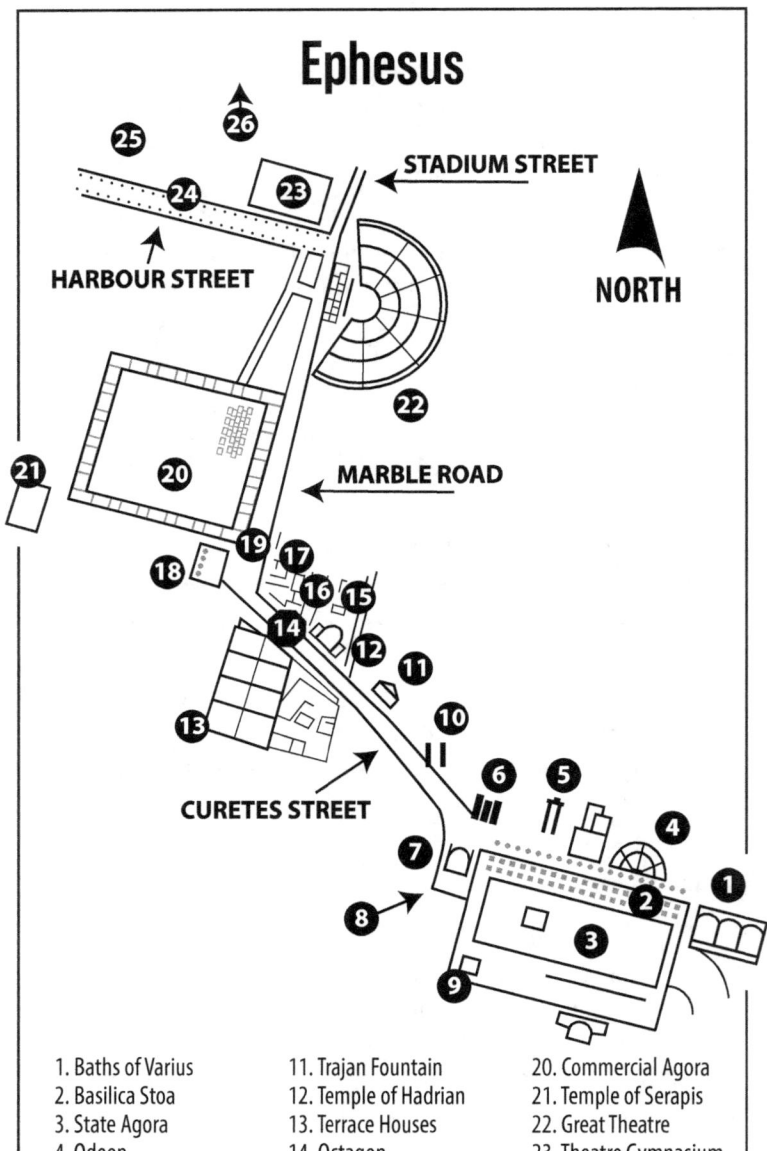

Ephesus

STADIUM STREET

HARBOUR STREET

NORTH

MARBLE ROAD

CURETES STREET

1. Baths of Varius
2. Basilica Stoa
3. State Agora
4. Odeon
5. Prytaneion
6. Memmius Monument
7. Temple of Domitian
8. Pollio Fountain
9. Water Palace
10. Gate of Hercules
11. Trajan Fountain
12. Temple of Hadrian
13. Terrace Houses
14. Octagon
15. Scholastica Baths
16. Public Toilets
17. Brothel
18. Library of Celsus
19. Gate of Mazaeus and
    Mithridates
20. Commercial Agora
21. Temple of Serapis
22. Great Theatre
23. Theatre Gymnasium
24. Column of the
    Evangelists
25. Harbour Baths
26. Church of St Mary

As you enter ancient Ephesus through the upper gate, some of the first structures you see are the three arches of the Baths of Varius. In seeing them, you get an idea of their impressive size.

— PHOTO BY DAVID KNIGHT

The baths — along with other structures in Ephesus — were destroyed by an earthquake in the 7th century. They have been excavated at various times between 1929 and 1979. Excavations and reconstructions are continuing in Ephesus.

Basilica Stoa (2) —

Constructed: 11 AD

On the north side of the State Agora are the ruins of the Basilica Stoa — sometimes called the Royal Portico. It was about 525 feet long and was built in 11 AD by C. Sextilius Pollio and his family. The stoa originally had two stories and three aisles. The columns were of the Ionic order.

Statues of Emperor Augustus and his wife Livia were discovered in the stoa. They are now on display in the Ephesus Museum.

State Agora (3) —

Constructed: 6th century BC

Located in the southeastern part of Ephesus near the upper gate, the State Agora was where politicians and citizens came to discuss government business. It is where law votes took place. The meetings were open to all citizens of Ephesus, including women and slaves.

The original agora was built in the 6th century BC. The current agora sits about six feet higher than the original agora.

In ancient times, Ephesus and Egypt enjoyed a good relationship. In the middle of the agora was a temple to the Egyptian goddess Isis. It featured pink marble columns. The temple was destroyed during the reign of Augustus, and some of the marble was used in the construction of the Pollio Fountain.

Archaeology excavations have discovered several tombs in the northeast area of the agora. These tombs date to the 7th and 6th century BC.

Although its glory days are long gone, the Odeon of Ephesus captures your attention with its marble seats and column remnants. Because the orchestra pit didn't have any drainage system, it is believed the Odeon was covered.

Odeon (4) —

Constructed: 150 AD

The Odeon still hosts concerts and special events today — some 2,000 years after it was built. This semi-circular theatre seats about 1,400 and was used for concerts, theatrical events, and other activities. It was also used for governmental business meetings.

Publius Vedius Antoninus and his wife funded the construction of the Odeon.

The word odeon means singing place. The structure is also known as the Bouleuterion because it was where the boule, or city council, met.

Prytaneion (5) —

Constructed: 3rd century BC

The Prytaneion held the sacred flame of Hestia, the goddess of fire. The flame represented the life and vitality of the city of Ephesus. The Prytaneion also was used as a city hall, and political discussions, banquets, and formal ceremonies were held there.

Excavations at the Prytaneion found two statues of Artemis which are now in the Ephesus Archaeological Museum. Among the remains are two Doric order columns.

Memmius Monument (6) —

Constructed: 30 BC

The Memmius Monument stands out against the blue sky.

In 88 BC, Mithridates, king of Pontus, captured Ephesus. A few years later, Roman General Lucius Cornelius Sulla Felix defeated Mithridates and took Ephesus. Gaius Memmius, grandson of Sulla Felix, built the Memmius Monument to pay tribute to this victory and to three generations of his family (including himself). Scholars believe the monument was designed as a four-sided victory arch.

In about 200, The Hydreion, was built adjacent to the monument. This fountain was financed by T. Flavius Meander.

Temple of Domitian (7) —

Constructed: 1st century AD

It is generally believed that this temple was built to honor Roman Emperor Domitian. However, some believe it was initially constructed to honor Titus. The temple was about 300 feet x 150 feet and had three levels.

The statue of Domitian, along with its base, stood about 27 feet tall. The head and arm of Domitian are on display in the Ephesus Museum. The altar of the temple is in the Izmir Museum.

Domitian opposed Christianity and persecuted Christians. He had the apostle John exiled to the Isle of Patmos. It was from there that John penned The Revelation.

On September 18, 96, Domitian was assassinated by court officials. He was 44.

Remnants of the Temple of Domitian (above) are a reminder of the tyrannical emperor who exiled John, the writer of The Revelation.

The Pollio Fountain (left) was one of several sources of fresh water in Ephesus.

— PHOTO BY DAVID KNIGHT

Pollio Fountain (8) —

Constructed: 97 AD

Just south of the State Agora is the Pollio Fountain which was built in 97 AD by C. S. Pollio and his family. It was built in memory of Sextillius Pollio who constructed the aqueduct which carried water to the city of Ephesus. Aqueducts carried water from as far away as the springs of Keltepe and Kenchiros which are south of Kuşadası, a distance of about 26 miles. Other springs that supplied water to Ephesus were Klaseas Spring and Selinus Spring.

The Pollio Fountain is opposite of the Temple of Domitian and was dedicated to the emperor.

Freshwater Pipes —

When water arrived in Ephesus via the aqueducts, it was then distributed by freshwater pipes. Around the city there are some stacks of these terra cotta pipes, and you may also see some *in situ*. Water to the Temple of Artemis came from the Selinus Spring, and site excavation discovered some thick lead pipes. One of these can be seen in the Ephesus Museum.

Water Palace (9) —

Constructed: 82 AD

The Water Palace, also referenced as The Hydrekdocheion or The Fountain of Laecanius Bassus, sits at the southwest corner of the State Agora. Gaius Laecanius Bassus ordered its construction while he was Governor of Ephesus. The fountain showcased the technology, architecture, and design skills of the Ephesians.

Gate of Hercules (10) —

Constructed: 4th century AD

The Gate of Hercules stands at the beginning of Curetes Street and was designed to prohibit chariot traffic thus making the street for pedestrian use only.

It is believed the structure was originally two stories tall featuring six columns on each floor. As you view the ruins, there are two columns, each with a relief of Hercules. On each he is depicted wearing the skin of a lion. In Greek mythology Hercules saved Nemea by destroying the lion which had plagued the region. These two columns have an inscription that dates them in the 2nd Century AD. In the building of the Gate of Hercules, they were recycled from an earlier structure.

Curetes Street —

As you pass the Gate of Hercules and start walking toward the Library of Celsus, a new world opens up. It is the main street of Ephesus, and one passes historic structure after historic structure. In ancient times people would walk this street going to the temple, heading to the market, or stopping in city hall to check about some political issue. However, as we view the remains of these magnificent structures, we need to remember that many of them were not there when Paul lived in Ephesus.

Curetes Street, along with Marble Road and Harbour Street, are the three main arteries of the city. In ancient Ephesus Curetes initially referred to priests and priestesses who served Artemis, but later they also had the responsibility of maintaining the sacred fire in the Prytaneion.

The Fountain of Trajan contained two ornate pools and was constructed in honor of Emperor Trajan by Tiberius Claudius Aristion.

Fountain of Trajan (11) —

Constructed: 114 AD

Trajan, along with Nerva, Hadrian, Antoninus Pius, and Marcus Aurelius, was recognized as one of the Five Good Emperors. They reigned from 96 to 180.

The monumental Fountain of Trajan contained two pools, and the upper pool was accented by Corinthian order columns. A statue of Trajan, which was twice the size of other statues, depicted his standing on a globe with water flowing under the statue. The inscription on the globe stated, "I have conquered it all, and it's now under my feet."

During excavations, statues of Aphrodite, Androklos, Dionysos, Nerva, and Satyr were discovered. These statues are in the Ephesus Museum.

Temple of Hadrian (12) —

Constructed: 138 AD

The Temple of Hadrian was built to honor this Roman Emperor who had twice visited the city of Ephesus. It was financed by P. Quintilius Valens Varius.

This magnificent arch showcases the exquisite design of the Temple of Hadrian.

— PHOTO BY DAVID KNIGHT

The temple was about 33 feet by 33 feet and had a height of about 25 feet with a barrel vault roof. Four Corinthian order columns highlight the front of the temple. Accenting the facade is an arch between the two center columns. Inside the temple is another arch featuring Medusa. The craftsmanship of the temple stands as a witness to the glory and artistic designs of ancient cities.

Belonging to the wealthy of the wealthy, there is an extra charge for visiting the Terrace Houses, but they are an impressive reminder of the financial status of many in Ephesus.

— PHOTO BY DALE W. MANOR

Terrace Houses (13) —

Constructed: Begun in the 1st century AD

These seven opulent residential buildings were homes to the richest Ephesians. Many floors have intricately designed mosaics, and frescoes on the walls have beautiful art with vibrant colors. Walking through the ruins — from the bedrooms to kitchens to dining rooms to reception halls — gives one a perspective of the "rich and famous" in Athens. Every nook and cranny has a story. They range in size from 1,000 square feet to 6,000 square feet.

Excavation of these houses began in 1960 under the direction of Hermann Vetters.

There is an additional charge for visiting the Terrace Houses.

Octagon (14) —

Construction: Late 1st century BC

Discovered in 1904, this eight-sided mausoleum dates back to the 1st Century BC. Excavations unearthed the tomb in 1929. Within it were the remains of a young lady in her mid to late teens.

Although the identity of the young lady is unknown, Hilke Thür of the Austrian Academy of Sciences suggested she might be Ptolemy Arsinoe IV, the youngest sister of Cleopatra.

Arsinoe IV was one of the last members of the Ptolemaic dynasty, and she took the title of Queen of Ptolemaic Egypt. She was an adversary of her sister (or half-sister) Cleopatra. After the siege of Alexandria in 47 BC, she was captured and taken to Rome. Later, she was exiled to the Temple of Artemis in Ephesus. It was there that she was executed on the steps of the temple by orders of Mark Antony, Cleopatra's lover.

Today, only the pedestal remains at the site. Following excavations in 1929, two columns and some of the relief fragments were taken to Austria. They are now on display in the Ephesus Museum in Vienna.

Scholastica Baths (15) —

Constructed: 1st century AD

Sites such as Scholastica Baths were the health spa of the day. One could go for their bath — perhaps beginning in an area similar to a sauna, proceeding to get an olive oil massage, and then taking time to relax and socialize later.

The original structure was built in the 1st Century AD. It was three stories tall and was said to be able to hold 1,000 people. There were three pools: cool, warm, and hot. It was heated by a hypocaust system, and parts of that system can still be seen today.

In the 4th Century, it was restored using stones from the Prytaneion. This restoration was funded by a wealth Christian lady named Scholastica. Scholastica's headless statue sits at the eastern entrance to the baths.

Public Toilets (16) —

Constructed: 1st century AD

Adjacent to Scholastica Baths are the public toilets. Most citizens did not have toilets in their homes, so having public toilets was a necessity. Marble benches lined three sides of the building. Each bench had 16 keyholes cut in them. Beneath the toilets was a channel which carried an uninterrupted flow of water.

Brothel (17) —

Constructed: 1st century AD

The Brothel was located near the intersection of Curetes Street and Marble Road and had entrances from both streets. The ground floor was the reception area, and it had a beautiful mosaic picturing the four seasons. There was an elliptical pool next to the reception center for guests to wash their hands and feet.

Along Curetes Street, there is a carving which is believed by many to be an advertisement for the Brothel.

Library of Celsus (18) —

Constructed: 135 AD

With 12,000 scrolls, the Library of Celsus was the third largest library in the world with only the Library of Alexandria and the Library of Pergamum eclipsing it.

The two story building was commissioned by Consul Gaius Julius Aquila to honor his father, Tiberius Julius Celsus Polemaeanus. Celsus was popular and wealthy, and he had served as Governor of the Roman province of Asia in 115.

The library's majestic design features a facade which is 69 feet wide and 56 feet tall. Sixteen marble columns topped with Corinthian order capitals accent the front portico. There are three front entrances to the building and statues of four Greek goddesses welcoming guests to the library. The four statues are Sophia, Arete, Ennoia, and Episteme, representing wisdom, virtue, thought, and knowledge respectively.

Other statues and reliefs adorn the building. The original statues are now in the Ephesus Museum in Vienna.

The structure also serves as a mausoleum for Celsus. Beneath the library is a crypt with an ornate white marble sarcophagus holding the remains of Celsus.

The library was destroyed by fire in 262. The facade remained intact, and in the late 4th Century, repairs were made to the library. In the 10th or 11th century, an earthquake destroyed the existing structure.

Throughout Ephesus are ruins of ancient structures waiting to be viewed by visitors or to be part of a reconstruction.

— PHOTOS BY KAY MILLS

In 1904, excavations by Austrian archaeologists discovered the sarcophagus of Celsus and parts of the library. In the 1970s, German archaeologist Volker Michael Strocka and Austrian architect Friedmund Hueber undertook the restoration of the library. This work concluded in 1978 and is what one sees today.

Gate of Mazaeus and Mithridates (19) —

Constructed: 3-2 BC

The stately three-arched Gate of Mazaeus and Mithridates bids one welcome to the Commercial Agora as they leave the area of the Library of Celsus. This triumphal triple arch was built by former slaves Mazaeus and Mithridates to honor Emperor Augustus because he gave them their freedom. After freeing the two, Augustus sent them to Ephesus and placed them in charge of managing properties which belonged to the Roman Empire in that area.

A rough translation of the dedicatory inscription on the arch reads: "From Emperor Caesar, Augustus, son of a god, the high priest, twelve times consul, twenty times tribune, and Livia, wife of Caesar Augustus, to Marc Agrippa, son of Lucius, three times consul, emperor, six times tribune and daughter of Julio Caesar Augustus, our patrons Mazeus and Mithridates"

In 1903, the gate was first excavated. Restoration took place from 1980-1989 using original pieces. Plaques inside the archway — one in Turkish and one in German — commemorate the reconstruction by the Austrian Archaeological Institute (ÖAI), under the directorship of H. Vetters and G. Langmann. Architectural research and project director: Friedmund Hueber. Initiator and financing: Anton Kallinger-Prskawetz.

The Commercial Agora in Ephesus is well defined. The lower photo shows small rail cars used to move artifacts.

Commercial Agora (20) —

Constructed: 300 BC

The Commercial Agora was the marketplace of Ephesus. It was the one place you could go to buy whatever you needed — food, clothing, home decor, furniture, leather goods, and silverware. Resident vendors who would be open on a regular schedule. There would be other vendors who might be there on a seasonal or "as needed" basis — such as we might have a farmer's market or garage sale.

The Agora was initially constructed about 300 BC during the Hellenistic period, but was rebuilt several times through the centuries. Rebuilding took place during the reign of Augustus and again during the reign of Nero. What was done during these reconstructions would be the Agora that Paul would see.

The Commercial Agora in Ephesus is about 360 feet by 360 feet — each side being longer than a football field. The north side was open but the other three sides were covered. In the middle was a courtyard and contained a sundial and water clock. The Ephesus Museum holds a 3rd century AD sundial that was discovered in the Agora.

When Paul was in Ephesus, he initially spoke for three months in the synagogue. After that, he continued "reasoning daily in the hall of Tyrannus" (Acts 19:9). This continued for two years.

The location of the hall of Tyrannus is not known, but some scholars believe it was in the area where the Library of Celsus was later built.

Paul was a tentmaker by trade (Acts 18:3), and he continued practicing this trade to financially support himself. When he wrote the Christians at Corinth (2 Corinthians 11:7-9) and Thessalonica (2 Thessalonians 3:7-9), he noted that he made it a point not to be a burden to them. This was possible for two reasons: 1) there were others who helped with his financial support, and 2) he continued to be a tentmaker to support himself.

In his time in Ephesus, it is reasonable to assume that he continued to make tents during the three years he was there. This would place him in the Agora working, visiting with people, discussing the scriptures, and teaching the gospel of Jesus Christ.

Temple of Serapis (21) —

Constructed: 2nd century AD

The Temple of Serapis, also known as the Serapeion of Ephesus, was built in the 2nd century AD to honor the Greco-Egyptian deity. The Temple is evidence of the strong trade ties Ephesus had with Egypt.

The complex contained a 328 feet by 246 feet terrace with the Corinthian-style temple being about 95 feet by 78 feet in size. Scholars question whether or not the temple was fully completed.

Because remains of a baptistry were found in the eastern corner, it is believed that the temple was converted into a Christian church during the 4th century.

Marble Road —

Construction: 1st century AD

Ephesus sits on the southwest side of Mount Pion (also known as Panayir Dağ), and Marble Road is part of a road that encircles the mount. It received that name because it was a section of the road that was covered with marble plates.

Looking down the Marble Road to the south, you can see the protective coverings for the Terrace Houses.

— PHOTO BY KAY MILLS

Marble Road runs between the Library of Celsus and the Great Theatre of Ephesus. During his reign, Emperor Nero converted the western side into a covered stoa. Along the way, there were busts and statues of important people.

It is said that the first ad appeared on Marble Road. There is a carving supposedly promoting a brothel. The carving pictures a left footprint (your foot must be this big to enter), a woman, a heart, a library, a purse of money, and a hole in the rock (you must have enough coins to fill this hole).

Great Theatre (22) —

Constructed: 3rd century BC

This magnificent theatre took 60 years to build while Lysimachus (who succeeded Alexander the Great) was king and is the largest ancient theatre in Türkiye. Initially, it was a Greek theatre, but later transformed into a Roman theatre. It rests on the slope of Mount Pion and can seat 25,000 people. During Paul's day it could seat about 12,000.

It is a marvel in acoustical engineering because one whispering from the stage can be clearly heard throughout the theatre. The three-story stage building is about 59 feet high.

Although larger today than in Paul's time, the Great Theatre of Ephesus would have still been an imposing site.

— PHOTO BY DAVID KNIGHT

The Theatre was used for community events, political discussions, religious ceremonies, and various types of entertainment.

As people arrived in Ephesus by ship and took Harbour Road to the city, the Great Theatre would be an imposing structure that would greet them. When the apostle Paul was in Ephesus, we have the record of his speaking in the synagogue and in the hall of Tyrannus, but we don't have any record of his speaking in the Great Theatre.

As Paul preached in Ephesus, he called people to Jesus Christ rather than Artemis. According to Demetrius, a silversmith, "Paul has persuaded and turned away a great many people, saying that gods made with hands are not gods" (Acts 19:26). The gathered craftsmen were enraged and began shouting "Great is Artemis of the Ephesians!" The word spread and people of Ephesus drug Paul's companions, Gaius and Aristarchus, to the Great Theatre. After some confusion, the crowd began to cry out, "Great is Artemis of the Ephesians!" For two solid hour they shouted as one voice, "Great is Artemis of the Ephesians!" Paul had preached in Ephesus for about three years, but after this event, he encouraged the disciples and then left for Macedonia.

This Great Theatre is still used for concerts today. Past performers include Ray Charles, Elton John, Jose Carreras, Diana Ross, Julio Iglesias, Bryan Adams, and Luciano Pavarotti. The International Ephesus Opera and Ballet Festival has taken place there since 2018.

Gymnasium (23) —

Constructed: 1st century AD

On Harbour Street immediately west of the Great Theatre is a gymnasium. It is one of several gymnasiums in this great city.

Harbour Street —

Harbour Street, also known as Arcadian Street, runs just about a third of a mile from the Ephesus Harbour to the Great Theatre of Ephesus. As ships docked, passengers and crew would be welcomed into the city by this thoroughfare which was graced with columns and statues.

Column of the Evangelists (24) —

Constructed: 6th century AD

Among the many columns on Harbour Street were four Corinthian order columns which are said to have once held statues of the four evangelists: Matthew, Mark, Luke, and John.

Harbour Baths (25) —

Constructed: 1st century AD

Located near the harbor entrance, these baths — according to some researchers — served two purposes: 1) to provide a place for travelers to bathe and freshen up, and 2) to provide a place for quarantine, if needed.

This is a three part complex consisting of the baths, a gymnasium, and athletic field.

These baths are off the beaten path, but there is a wide variety of ruins for those who want to make their way to the site.

Church of St Mary (26) —

There is speculation that the Church of St Mary — sometimes called the Church of the Council — was built for the Third Ecumenical Council, the Council of Ephesus, which met in 431. One of the major discussions of the council was whether to refer to Mary as the Mother of God or the Mother of Christ.

The sanctuary was about 475 feet by 98 feet. On the north side of the west end was a circular immersion baptistry. It is said that thousands of pagans were baptized here. Because the church has been rebuilt a number of times over the centuries, what you see today is not as it was in 431. The site had been home to an earlier building, Hall of the Muses, where lectures and debates were held. It was destroyed by fire.

— House of Virgin Mary —

37.9115700,27.3340190 / 37° 54′ 41.652″ N 27° 20′ 2.468″ E

Constructed: 4th century AD / Foundation possibly 1st century AD

The House of the Virgin Mary is a small brick and stone one-story house on Mount Nightingale (Bülbüldağı in Turkish) about 3 miles south of ancient Ephesus. It is viewed as a modest chapel today. There is a keyhole baptismal pool as you approach the house.

This keyhole baptistry is just a short distance from the House of Mary.

— PHOTO BY KAY MILLS

The House of Mary is a beautiful stone structure.

— PHOTO BY NOEL WHITLOCK

As Jesus was hanging on the cross, he saw the apostle John standing nearby and said to his mother, "Woman, behold your son!" Then he looked at John and said, "Behold, ycur mother!" John then took the mother of Jesus to his house (John 19:26-27). Many believe that John took care of Mary for the rest of her life.

It is generally agreed that this John is the apostle of love and the author of the gospel of John, the epistles bearing his name, and The Revelation.

Irenaeus of Lyons, a 2nd century church father and one who learned from Polycarp, wrote *Against Heresies (Adversus Haereses)* about 180 AD. He stated that John lived and ministered in Ephesus until Trajan's reign (98-117 AD). He wrote, "Then John, the disciple of the Lord, who also had leaned upon His breast, did himself publish a Gospel during his residence at Ephesus in Asia" (*Against Heresies* 3.1.1).

Tradition says that Mary had gone to Ephesus with John and that she died there either 43 or 48. Others believe that Mary lived out her life in Jerusalem.

John was later exiled to Patmos where he wrote the Revelation. Before his death, he returned to Ephesus and is believed to be buried where the Basilica of St John was built.

— Ephesus Archaeological Museum —
37.9489431, 27.3678689 / 37° 56' 56.195" N 27° 22' 4.328" E

Artifacts from earlier archaeological expeditions at Ephesus wound up in other nations. Items discovered between 1867 and 1905 are in the British Museum. The Ephesus Museum in Vienna, Austria, house discoveries found between 1905 and 1923. On October 23, 1923, after the Turkish War of Independence and with the leadership of Mustafa Kemal Atatürk, the Republic of Turkey was established. The new republic enacted a law which forbade taking artifacts out of the country.

In 1929, a warehouse was built to protect antiquities discovered in Ephesus and the surrounding area. In 1964, the Ephesus Archaeological Museum was founded. It is home to over 60,000 artifacts.

When you visit the museum, you will see that objects are categorized according to item type and not chronologically. There are various halls including residential relics, recent finds, funerary relics, gladiators, imperial cults and portraits, stone artifacts, fountain relics, and others.

— Basilica of St John —

37.9525490, 27.3679540 / 37° 57′ 9.176″ N 27° 22′ 4.634″ E

After returning from his exile to Patmos, tradition says that the apostle John spent his last years around Ephesus living on a hill which became known as Hagia Theologos — "Holy Theologian." It was later named Ayasuluk Hill. The apostle is thought to have been about 98 years old when he died and that he was buried near where he lived.

The Basilica of St John is between the Temple of Artemis and Aysuluk Castle. It is in the shape of a cross and was built over what is believed to be the grave of John (above).

— PHOTO BY DALE W. MANOR

A small chapel was constructed over his grave about 300 years after his death. In the 6th century, Byzantine Emperor Justinian built a cruciform basilica over the grave. The basilica was constructed of stone and brick, and it featured six domes. North of the nave is an immersion keyhole baptistry which was built in the 5th or 6th century.

— Ayasuluk Castle —

37.9551390, 27.3680390 / 37° 57′ 18.500″ N 27° 22′ 4.940″ E

Overlooking the Basilica of St John and the city of Selçuk is Ayasuluk Castle. It was constructed in the 6th century by the Byzantines using recycled stones from Greek and Roman buildings. The massive walls have 15 watchtowers. There are two gates: the west gate, which is used for tourists, and an east gate. Additional defensive walls came down the hill and surrounded the Basilica of St John.

— Grotto of St Paul —

37.9383488, 27.3344567 / 37° 56' 18.056" N 27° 20' 4.044" E

On the south side of ancient Ephesus is the Grotto of St Paul. It is about 50 feet long, 7-1/2 feet high, and 6-1/2 feet wide. The cave has been sacred to Christians since the latter part of the 1st century or first part of the 2nd century. A back room served as a chapel for these Christians.

Inside the Grotto of St Paul are several frescoes. The most striking piece is one of the apostle Paul teaching. To his left is Theocleia, and to his right is her daughter, Thecla, listening through an open window (not shown).

— PHOTO BY DAVID KNIGHT

It is believed that local shepherds used the cave over the centuries.

While looking for the tomb of Mary, two priests, Henri Jung and Eugene Poulin, discovered the cave. In 1906, the Austrian Archaeological Institute explored the cave. Karl Herold discovered some frescoes beneath the plaster on the walls.

Within the cave are numerous frescoes including Elisha taking up the mantle of Elijah, a scene with four rivers, and Abraham and Isaac. In 1999, a painting of the apostle Paul preaching was discovered by Dr. Renate Pillinger from the University of Vienna. On Paul's right is Thecla (an early disciple) leaning out of a window listening to him preach. On his left is Theocleia, Thecla's mother.

The Grotto of St Paul is not normally open for the public, but guides can periodically get permission to take people to the site.

Dr. Dale W. Manor is just a short distance from the Grotto of St Paul. In the background, you can see the Great Theatre of Ephesus in the upper left. — PHOTO BY DAVID KNIGHT

This cat was photographed near the Temple of Domitian. Dr. Dale W. Manor commented, "It's sitting there as smug as can be. Of course — it's a cat!" — PHOTO BY DALE W. MANOR

— Cats of Ephesus —

As one walks through Ephesus admiring the antiquities and being in awe of ancient craftsmanship, you can't help but notice all the cats. Cats have their own kingdom in Ephesus. They are fat, sassy, and — for the most part — enjoy the attention given by visitors.

In much of the ancient world cats were revered and protected, and in some cases, they were considered sacred. Cats protected crops and killed predators. There are several examples of cat-headed deity.

Sabine Ladstätter (1968-2024) was Director of the Austrian Archaeological Institute (ÖAI) from 2009 to 2024 and managed the archaeological excavations in Ephesus for a number of years. She, along with Lois Lammerhuber and Niki Gail, wrote a book, *Cats of Ephesos.*

— Temple of Artemis —
37.9495636, 27.3639381 / 37° 56′ 58.429″ N 27° 21′ 50.177″ E

— PHOTO BY DAVID KNIGHT

I have set eyes on the wall of lofty Babylon on which is a road for chariots, and the statue of Zeus by the Alpheus, and the hanging gardens, and the colossus of the Sun, and the huge labour of the high pyramids, and the vast tomb of Mausolus; but when I saw the house of Artemis that mounted to the clouds, those other marvels lost their brilliancy, and I said, 'Lo, apart from Olympus, the Sun never looked on aught so grand.'   — Antipater of Sidon, *Greek Anthology* (IX.58)

What once was The Grand Temple of Artemis is now a small area of ruins. (Artemis is her Greek name; Diana is her Roman name). There is one reconstructed column standing which is made up of mismatched drums. Located about 2,500 yards northeast of ancient Ephesus and down the hill from Ayasuluk Castle, the Temple of Artemis was once one of the Seven Wonders of the Ancient World.

Worship of Artemis in this temple area goes back to the 10th century BC. A small simple temple was constructed in the 7th century BC. Around 570 BC, King Croesus of the Lydian Kingdom funded the construction of a grander temple.

Croesus' temple was destroyed by fire in 356 BC. It is believed by many that a person named Herostratus started the fire in order to gain fame. One legend says that it burned on the day of the birth of Alexander the Great and that Artemis was too busy paying attention to his birth to protect her temple.

When Alexander the Great liberated Ephesus in 334 BC, he offered to fund the rebuilding of the temple. The people of Ephesus rejected his offer because they did not believe it proper for one god to build a temple to another god.

After Alexander's death in 323 BC, the people of Ephesus began rebuilding the Temple of Artemis. It had about 127 structural columns which were 60 feet tall. This most palatial and glorious temple was about four times larger than the Parthenon in Athens. It stood for about 600 years.

It's ruins were discovered by John Turtle Wood on December 31, 1869. Because Wood was funded by the British Museum, many of the grand artifacts are in London. Eight magnificent green columns from the temple are a part of the Hagai Sophia in Istanbul, Türkiye.

Reflections —

One thing I really like about the church at Ephesus is that it gives us a life perspective no other New Testament church offers. There are three chapters in the life of the church at Ephesus:

Ephesus was
> 1. A Following Church (Acts 19:1-20:1; 20:17-38)
> 2. A Faithful Church (Paul's letter to the church)
> 3. A Falling Church (Jesus' letter to the church: Revelation 2:1-7)

As a Following Church...

When Paul first visited Ephesus, he met disciples and taught them about the baptism of Jesus. He taught publicly in the synagogue and the Hall of Tyrannus "reasoning and persuading them about the kingdom of God" (Acts 19:8). The new disciples were mentored in Christian living and in evangelism by Paul as "all the residents of Asia heard the word of the Lord" (Acts 19:10), and they were growing.

As a Faithful Church...

Paul wrote the Christians at Ephesus several years after he ministered there. His letter — although only six chapters long — is a wealth of teaching, encouragement, hope, and blessing. Martyn Lloyd-Jones, who preached at Westminster in London 1939-1968, was an expository preacher who preached a series of 232 sermons on the book of Ephesians. It is a rich book.

Paul commended them for their faith and love. There are several themes that stand out, but let's notice these three:

- ◆ The wonderful blessings "in Him" in 1:3-14.
- ◆ The unifying "ones" elements in 4:1-6.
- ◆ The calling to be armed in the strength of the Lord 6:10-20. Notice that the outfitting of armor ends with a call to prayer.

Throughout the book, Paul sprinkles thoughts about love, faithfulness, Christian living, relationships, belonging, doctrine, hope...

He reminds them of their calling in Christ Jesus —

"For by grace you have been saved through faith. And this is not your own doing; it is the gift of God, not a result of works, so that no one may boast. For we are his workmanship, created in Christ Jesus for good works, which God prepared beforehand, that we should walk in them" (Ephesians 2:8-10).

He appealed to the Father for their faithfulness —

"For this reason I bow my knees before the Father, from whom every family in heaven and on earth is named, that according to the riches of his glory he may grant you to be strengthened with power through his Spirit in your inner being, so that Christ may dwell in your hearts through faith—that you, being rooted and grounded in love, may have strength to comprehend with all the saints what is the breadth and length and height and depth, and to know the love of Christ that surpasses knowledge, that you may be filled with all the fullness of God" (Ephesians 3:14-19)

He gave praise to the Father for His holy power —

"Now to him who is able to do far more abundantly than all that we ask or think, according to the power at work within us, to him be glory in the church and in Christ Jesus throughout all generations, forever and ever. Amen" (Ephesians 3:20-21).

One outstanding book about Paul's letter is Watchman Nee's inspiring book *Sit, Walk, Stand* in which he notes the apostle's message is the call to Christian maturity.

The letter to this group of Christians is encouraging because we see disciples who are committed to the calling of Jesus Christ

As a Falling Church...

A number of years later, things had changed at Ephesus. As Jesus wrote them in The Revelation, He commended them, but He also rebuked them, "But I have this against you, that you have abandoned the love you had at first" (Revelation 2:4). I believe the New Living Translation gives this verse a fresh perspective: "You don't love me or each other as you did at first!"

I believe they were still meeting; they were still fellowshipping; they were still singing; they were still communing together — but priorities had changed. Other things had become more important. Jesus no longer held first place in their lives.

In writing the Christians at Corinth, Paul reminded them that God has given us the ministry of reconciliation (2 Corinthians 5:16-21).

Jesus then directs the Christians at Ephesus to this ministry of reconciliation and called them to look inwardly and see their need to be reconciled to Him — to again make Him first in their lives.

His reconciliation advice:

◆ **Remember** the faith and love they once had.

◆ **Repent** of their sins, shortcomings, and apathy.

◆ **Return** to living as they had earlier. Be the faithful saint.

This advice that Jesus gave to the church at Ephesus is important for us today. It is a pattern by which we can take inventory in our faith life, in our personal life, in our marriage, in our family — maybe even in our community service and in our business.

Chapter 27

Miletus – A Final Farewell

37.5302260, 27.2745760 / 37° 31′48.814″ N 27° 16′28.474″ E

Located in modern-day Türkiye, Miletus is an ancient Greek city less than an hour south of Kuşadası, Türkiye, just over an hour south of the biblical city of Ephesus, and near the municipality of Didim.

In ancient times, Miletus sat on a peninsula in the Latmian Gulf. The gulf was fed by the Büyük Mende- res River, sometimes called the Maeander River. Lion's Harbor was aptly named because it was guarded by sculptures of two lions.

It dates to the Neolithic period and reflects Greek influence during the 11th century BC. Miletus came to prominence in the 7th and 6th centuries BC.

Paul and his fellow evangelists had been in Troas. They were headed to Miletus and then on to Jerusalem. As his companions sailed, Paul chose to walk and meet them in Assos — a distance of about 31 miles. This would have taken Paul the better part of two days. Above are the remains of the Roman road near Apollon Smintheion that people can still walk.

— PHOTO BY DALE W. MANOR

The question comes up about why Paul wanted to walk this distance. Were there people he knew along the way? Was he looking for opportunities to meet people and share the gospel? Did he just need time to be by himself? Did he want to spend some private time in prayer with God knowing he had a difficult and emotional meeting coming up in Miletus with the Ephesian elders?

Paul in Miletus —

At the end of his third missionary journey, the apostle Paul wanted to visit with the elders of Ephesus, but he also wanted to get to Jerusalem by Pentecost. If he stopped at Ephesus, a couple of things might happen: 1) because of his love for the church there his stay would probably be longer than intended, and 2) he would see opportunities for evangelism and continue to teach for a period of time. This means he wouldn't get to Jerusalem by Pentecost.

Because of this, he proceeded to Miletus and sent for the Ephesian elders. It was a meeting Paul desired to have because he wanted to encourage the elders and the church at Ephesus. Yet, I'm sure it was a meeting Paul dreaded because he knew it was probably the last time he would see these beloved brethren.

Within the text in Acts 20:13-38, we see the:
◆ Calling of the elders (v. 17)
◆ Compelling call to ministry (vv. 18-24)
◆ Charging the elders (vv. 25-31)
◆ Commending the elders to God (vv. 32-35)
◆ Concluding in prayer (vv. 36-38)

Other Biblical References —

The only other time Miletus is mentioned in the Bible is in 2 Timothy 4:20. As Paul concluded his letter to Timothy, he mentioned leaving Trophimus at Miletus because of illness. Trophimus was with Paul on his third missionary journey (Acts 20:4), and he was with him after they returned to Jerusalem (Acts 21:29). Because Paul stated he left Trophimus in Miletus, they must have been traveling together on Paul's journey to Rome (Acts 27-28).

Archaeological Excavations —

In 1873, French researcher Olivier Rayet began excavation work in Miletus. A German team of Julius Hülsen and Theodor Wiegand continued the work from 1899-1931. A team from Ruhr-Universität Bochum in Bochum, Germany, currently conducts excavations in Miletus.

In the early 1900s, the marble market gate, which is almost 100 feet wide and just over 50 feet tall, was unearthed, rebuilt, and placed in the Pergamon Museum in Berlin, Germany.

Sites to See —

Theatre of Miletus (1) —

Initially built by the Greeks in the 4th century BC, the Theatre of Miletus was expanded in the 1st century AD by the Romans when Trajan was Emperor. The Romans increased the seating capacity to about 15,000 people. The diameter of the seating area is about 450 feet, and the theatre has excellent acoustics. It is the best preserved structure in Miletus.

The Theatre of Miletus is the best preserved structure in the city. From the top tier, you have a great panoramic view of the area.

— PHOTO BY DAVID KNIGHT

İlyas Bey Kervansarayı (2) —

This was the Holiday Inn of years gone by. Believed to have been built about 1800, it had several rooms which surrounded a courtyard. It also contained a stable for animals.

Miletus

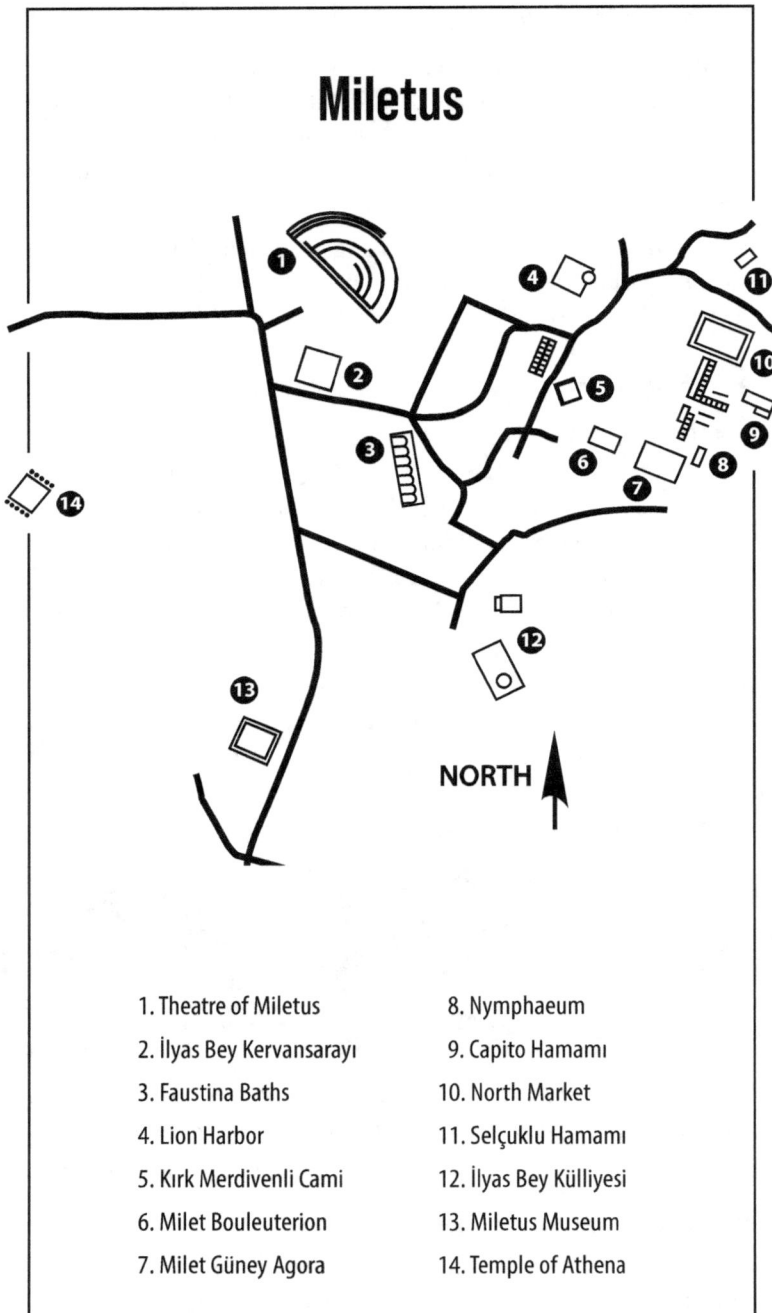

NORTH

1. Theatre of Miletus
2. İlyas Bey Kervansarayı
3. Faustina Baths
4. Lion Harbor
5. Kırk Merdivenli Cami
6. Milet Bouleuterion
7. Milet Güney Agora
8. Nymphaeum
9. Capito Hamamı
10. North Market
11. Selçuklu Hamamı
12. İlyas Bey Külliyesi
13. Miletus Museum
14. Temple of Athena

Faustina Baths (3) —

The Faustina Baths were constructed around the middle of the 2nd century and were named in honor of Roman empress Faustina. These baths are rather large and rather well preserved for ancient ruins. When using the baths, one would progress from the frigidarium (cold room) to the tepidarium (warm room) and then to the caladarium (hot room).

Great Harbor Monument at Lion Bay (4) —

During antiquity, Miletus had four harbors. Lion's Harbor was perhaps the most strategic harbor. Two marble lions, which dated back to the 3rd century BC, guarded the harbor entrance. Was this where Paul's ship docked? We don't know. As you view the harbor and the city, know that it was in this area where the Ephesian elders accompanied him to the ship. There they prayed and had their emotional farewells as they realized they would never see him again.

Kırk Merdivenli Cami (5) —

Just a few wall remain from this 14th century mosque and bath complex. Its name means Forty Stairs Mosque, and very little is known about it.

Milet Bouleuterion (6) —

The Bouleuterion at Miletus — or Council House — dates to the 2nd century BC, and it was funded by Seleucid king Antiochus IV Epiphanes. A boule is a council or parliament. As you entered through an impressive vestibule, you walked into the stately courtyard. You then went into the assembly hall which had semi-circular seating and could accommodate up to 1,200 people. The total structure was about 114 feet by 184 feet.

Milet Güney Agora (7) —

This once-large complex was the South Agora and dated back to the 3rd century BC. The market gate dates to the 2nd century AD. It measured about 417 feet by 530 feet. Its gate was about 100 feet wide, 52 feet tall, and 16 feet deep. It was a two-story structure and had three entrances. After it was discovered by a team of German archaeologists in the early 1900s, it was excavated and taken to Berlin. It was reconstructed and is now in the Pergamon Museum in Berlin.

Nymphaeum (8) —

This elaborate Roman fountain was constructed during the 2nd century AD. It was an ornate three story structure that collected water from several sources and supplied it to the city.

Capito Hamamı (9) —

These Roman baths are the most ancient in Miletus and date from the 1st century. They were named after Gnaeus Vergilius Capito who was the Roman governor of Egypt at this time while Claudius was Roman Emperor (41-54 AD).

North Market of Miletus (10) —

Dating back to the 5th century BC, the North Agora was the oldest of the agoras in Miletus. It developed into the "town square" as there were official buildings, commercial businesses, and an open square where people could assemble.

Selçuklu Hamamı (11) —

This bathhouse was built for the ancient city of Miletus by the Turkish principalities that settled in the region after the Byzantine Empire. It has not been restored and is in ruins. Everything can be brought to light by much more detailed excavations and research in the city.

İlyas Bey Külliyesi (Complex) (12) —

Located just outside the city walls of Miletus, this complex is named for its founder, İlyas Bey, which means Mr. Elijah. It dates to the early 1400s, and the largest building is the mosque. There are other buildings, a cemetery, and two bath houses. Beginning in 2008, it was restored over a period of three years.

Miletus Museum (13) —

This museum of almost 13,000 square feet opened in May 2011. Most of the items in it come from Miletus, but some come from the surrounding area. You will see jewelry, ceramics, statues, and other objects of interest. The oldest items are from the Minoan civilization.

Temple of Athena (14) —

The Temple of Athena at Miletus (Milet Athena Tapınağı) was constructed during the 5th century BC, and is the oldest temple in Miletus. Only the foundation, which is about 59 feet by 115 feet, remains today. About two centuries earlier, a smaller temple to Athena had-been built on the same site. Just north of the temple was the West Agora which was built in the 2nd century BC.

Reflections —

Although Paul's stop at Miletus was just a "roadside stop" to make a somewhat quick visit with the elders from Ephesus, there are a couple of things to note:

1. There are times we must pause and reflect on our relationship with our Lord and Savior Jesus Christ and with others. Paul was calling on the elders of Ephesus to do just that.

2. There will come a day when we will say goodbye to our loved ones and best of friends. Paul and the elders knew this was that day. For most of us, we don't know when that day will be, so let's live with love, respect, and faithfulness every day so we don't have any regrets.

Looking toward the east and viewing the northwest corner of the Theatre of Miletus, you notice the stairway and several arched openings.

— PHOTO BY DAVID KNIGHT

Chapter 28

Islands of Greece – Ancient Charm

Greek islands are some of the most wonderful places to visit. Many of the islands are rich in history and culture. Some are a collection of rugged outcroppings. Hiking and biking trails abound. Among the islands you'll found some of the most stunning beaches in the world, and they are touching the crystal clear blue Aegean Sea. You can swim, and you can sail. Islands on the western side of Greece are surrounded by the Ionian Sea.

There are about 6,000 Greek islands and islets. Maybe 200-225 are inhabited.

In reading the record of the apostle Paul's travels, very few of these islands are mentioned although he would have sailed by an unknown number of islands.

There are six groups of islands. Sometimes islands are identified as to which group they belong. Sometimes the islands are mentioned by name. However, of the 6,000 islands, maybe only a few names are recognizable to most of us: Santorini, Mykonos, Crete, Corfu, Patmos, Samothrace, Rhodes, Samos…

The largest island is Crete, and it is home to the Minoan civilization. Paul made a stop there on his way to Rome. Santorini has an aura of being a romantic island with magical sunsets. People enjoy the windmills of Mykonos.

As you visit islands of Greece — whether from a cruise ship, on a guided tour, or as you travel on your own — there are enchanting sites to see, history to be learned, picturesque landscapes to photograph, and a plethora of events in which to participate.

Chapter 29

Islands of Paul – Safe Shelters

My Granddad Layton grew up around Reagor Springs, Texas, a little bit south of Dallas. In 1908, when he was 16, Mr. Charlie Osborne sent him to West Texas to meet a man with some mules. His journey took a couple of weeks over dusty trails and dirt roads. He wouldn't have found many paved or brick roads — if any.

I'm not sure Granddad's journey was much different than what the apostle Paul would have encountered, although Paul did have some excellent roadways for the day, such as the Via Egnatia. As people did in ancient days, Paul traveled overland on whatever roads and trails were available, and he sailed on the seas to get to his destinations.

Paul's Second Missionary Journey —

In looking at Paul's second missionary journey, the record lists four times he traveled by ship: 1) From Troas to Neapolis; 2) Leaving Berea, going to the coast and sailing to Athens; 3) Sailing from Cenchrea to Ephesus; and 4) Sailing from Ephesus to Caesarea Maritima.

Undoubtedly, Paul sailed by a number of islands, but only one is mentioned by name. As Paul and his companions sailed from Troas to Neapolis, they overnighted in Samothrace. We covered this stop on page 37, Chapter 4.

Paul's Third Missionary Journey —

On the apostle's third journey, more islands are mentioned. They give us a perspective of Paul's travels and how the islands played a vital role in the lives of sailors during this period of time.

As Paul and his companions (Luke, Sopater, Aristarchus, Secundus, Gaius, Timothy, Tychicus, and Trophimus) were heading back to Jerusalem, they went to Troas where they stayed for seven days. This allowed them to fellowship with the Christians in that area, encourage them, and share communion with them on the first day of the week. When they met, Paul preached. You probably remember that during his sermon a young man went to sleep and fell out the window.

As they left Troas, Paul's companions boarded the ship and sailed to Assos where they were to pick up Paul. For some reason Paul wanted to travel overland to Assos. The distance between the two cities is about 21 miles as the crow flies. The Roman road between the two cities — which is still in pretty good condition — makes the distance about 31 miles. This journey would probably have taken Paul the better part of two days. I'm just wondering if there were people along the way that Paul wanted to visit, if he was taking the journey to seek new opportunities to teach the gospel, if he just needed to be by himself and have some private time with God…

Paul met the ship in Assos, and they sailed to Mitylene, which is the capital city and port of Lesbos, the third-largest Greek island.

The island of Samos is just about a mile from the coast of Türkiye. Separating the two is the Mycale Strait through which Paul and his companions would probably have sailed. On some of the cruises today, the ship leaves the harbor at Kuşadası and passes through the Mycale Strait on its way to Patmos.

The text mentions the other islands: "And sailing from there we came the following day opposite Chios; the next day we touched at Samos; and the day after that we went to Miletus" (Acts 20:15).

As they sailed from Assos to Miletus, they stayed close to what is modern-day Türkiye. The fact that these islands belong to Greece but are rather close to the Republic of Türkiye creates somewhat of a tension between the two nations.

After they left Miletus, the Bible states, "And when we had parted from them and set sail, we came by a straight course to Cos, and the next day to Rhodes, and from there to Patara" (Acts 21:1). After Patara, they continued their journey to Jerusalem.

Patara was an ancient maritime city that, at one point, was capital of Lycia. The Greek islands that are referenced in this journey are Lesbos (Mitylene), Chios, Samos, Cos, and Rhodes. This is the only time these islands are mentioned in the Bible, and the ship would have stopped there for an overnight anchorage.

Paul's Journey to Rome —

Even though Paul had not been to Rome, he was in touch with the Christians there and wrote them. He had a heart for these saints and longed to visit them (Romans 1:8-15). When he finally made the journey to Rome, it probably was not as he had envisioned since he was going there as a prisoner. However, that door was opened to him — no matter the circumstances — and he ministered to people in Rome. He also continued to mentor those he had met, taught, and encouraged on his earlier journeys as he wrote Colossians, Ephesians, Philemon, and Philippians from Rome.

Before Paul journeyed to Rome, he had already faced difficulties as an apostle. Among his listings was this statement: "Three times I was beaten with rods. Once I was stoned. Three times I was shipwrecked; a night and a day I was adrift at sea" (2 Corinthians 11:25). These experiences — as well as his being led by the Holy Spirit — would benefit him on this most difficult journey to Rome.

Acts 27 records this voyage. Phrases describing this trip include "the winds were against us," "the wind did not allow us," "the voyage was now dangerous," "the harbor was not suitable to spend the winter in," "we were violently storm-tossed," "without food for a long time"…

But God — through Paul — gave them hope: "As day was about to dawn, Paul urged them all to take some food, saying, 'Today is the fourteenth day that you have continued in suspense and without food, having taken nothing. Therefore I urge you to take some food. For it will give you strength, for not a hair is to perish from the head of any of you.' And when he had said these things, he took bread, and giving thanks to God in the presence of all he broke it and began to eat. Then they all were encouraged and ate some food themselves" (Acts 27:33-36).

In reading about this journey to Rome in Acts 27, there are only two islands mentioned: Crete and Cauda. They traveled along the southern shore of Crete, and these locations are mentioned: Salmone, Fair Haven (near Lasea), and Phoenix.

Caude, now known as Gavdos, is a small island south of Crete and is the southernmost Greek island and is also the southernmost point of Europe.

Of these few islands mentioned during Paul's journeys, Luke writes more about Crete than any other one. But it seems there was a story of God's providence that needed to be told. And it was a mighty story. The other islands? It looks like they didn't have any great stories. However, at a time when Paul and his companions needed it, they provided safe shelters. And isn't that what we need in life a lot of times?

Chapter 30

Islands of the Sea – Making Memories

Tourism and shipping are two of the biggest economic factors on the islands of Greece. Agriculture, particularly olives and grapes, benefit the economy of some islands. You will also find that fishing and small manufacturing companies make their contributions.

Islands in Greece have hosted filmmakers over the years. *Mamma Mia!* was filmed on the Greek islands of Skopelos and Skiathos. Filming sites for *Boy on a Dolphin*, which starred Alan Ladd, Clifton Webb, and Sophia Loren, included the islands of Hydra, Rhodes, and Delos. *The Guns of Navarone* starred Gregory Peck and Anthony Quinn and was filmed on Rhodes for the most part. Another Anthony Quinn movie was *Zorba the Greek*, and it was filmed on Crete.

Corfu, Crete, Mykonos, Rhodes, and Santorini are some of the most visited islands.

Santorini has a population of a little over 15,000 people, and about 3,400,000 people visit this island each year. There are some 800 or so cruise ship stops during the year, and other visitors arrive by ferry or commercial flights.

Mykonos hosts about 1,500,000 tourists a year. Crete and Rhodes each have several million visitors every year. An untold number visit other islands.

These islands have enormous marketing budgets promoting themselves as tourism destinations. Yet, these same tourists create a strain on the infrastructure, so on July 1, 2025, Greece instituted a new tax for cruise ship passengers to cover maintenance.

A couple of things to note: 1) This is not the first tourist tax Greece has enacted, and 2) These taxes are not going to stop people from visiting these magnificent islands.

Many tours focusing on the apostle Paul's missionary journeys include a few days on a ship for a 3- or 4-day — or even longer — cruise. That's how a large percentage of groups visit Ephesus, and it also gives people the opportunity to visit some of the magical Greek islands not mentioned in the Bible.

At each port call, there are excursions you can take. Some of these excursions may be included in your group tour; other stops allow you to choose from other various excursions.

Depending on the cruise line and the ship, you may have the opportunity for a behind-the-scenes ship tour to visit the bridge and operational areas. Some ships have a spa, pickle ball courts, swimming pools, and theatres with evening shows.

Let's take a brief look at some of the islands. This will give you an idea of some of the sites you can see, and excursions you can take — maybe as a part of your group tour, perhaps a cruise ship option, by private tour, or by striking out on your own. When you visit any location, if you have the option to choose your own tour/activity, research and see all your various options.

In this chapter, two of the islands are a part of the biblical storyline: Crete and Patmos. We see Paul's ship sought shelter at three harbors in Crete as they were traveling to Rome. We also see that he communicated with Titus about the church in Crete.

As far as we know, Paul never stopped at Patmos. However, this is where the apostle John wrote The Revelation, and cruise ships make a stop at the island.

— Chios —

38.3687755, 26.1358129 / 38° 22′ 7.592″ N 26° 8′ 8.926″ E

Along with five or six other places, Chios claims to be the birthplace of the author Homer. **The Daskalopetra** (Stone of the Teacher) in Vrontados (38.4218169,26.1349442 / 38° 25′ 18.541″ N 26° 8′ 5.799″ E) is the traditional site of where Homer was seated when reciting his poem for students to transcribe.

Chios is the fifth largest Greek island and sits in the Aegean Sea about four miles west of Türkiye and about 50 miles due west of Izmir, Türkiye. It is about 325 square miles and home to over 50,000 people.

These four traditional windmills accent the beauty of the bay.

— PHOTO BY NANTO / PIXABAY

Archaeology in Chios —

Archaeological excavations display evidence of inhabitants as far back as the Neolithic period. Prominent archaeologists in Chios included Spyridon Marinatos who worked in the early to mid 20th century. Sinclair Hood worked with the British School of Archaeology at Athens. In 1952, he began excavating the ruins of Emporio.

In the 1960s Christos G. Doumas began working in the Cyclades, but his work also included research relating to Chios which is a part of the North Aegean group of islands.

Sites to See —

The Nea Moni Monastery —

38.3740047, 26.0559967 / 38° 22′ 26.417″ N   26° 3′ 21.588″ E

This monastery dates from the 11th century. It houses an impressive number of mosaics and was once home to 800 monks. During the Greek War of Independence in 1822, over 2,000 people sought refuge in the monastery. The Ottomans attacked it, slaughtered many people, and burned the building. This event is depicted in a painting, "The Massacre of Chios," by French artist Eugène Delacroix, and it hangs in the Louvre in Paris.

Chios Windmills —

38.3823430,26.1383369 / 38° 22′ 56.435″ N 26° 8′ 18.013″ E)

Four traditional windmills are located on the road to Vrontados.

Archaeological Site of Emporios —

38.1948516, 26.0282558 / 38° 11′ 41.466″ N   26° 1′ 41.721″ E

Located on the hill of Prophet Elias, the Archaeological Site of Emporios dates back to the 8th century BC. In 1952, British archaeologist Martin Sinclair Frankland Hood began excavations at the site and continued until 1955. Various residences and buildings, as well as the Temple of Athena (38.1928683, 26.0309138 / 38° 11′ 34.326″ N   26° 1′ 51.290″ E) were discovered.

The Castle of Chios —

38.3717159, 26.1366319 / 38° 22′ 18.177″ N   26° 8′ 11.875″ E

The Castle of Chios is located next to the harbor and dates from medieval times having been built by the Byzantines around the 10th century.

Chios City Tour —

Enjoy a bus tour which stops at a number of important and historical sites in Chios including the fortified Castle of Chios, Chios Maritime Museum which showcases the nautical history of Chios, the Archaeological Museum of Chios, the Chios Mastic Museum, the Osmaniye Mosque, and the Monastery of our Lady Help.

Beaches of Chios —

There are beaches all around Chios. Some are sandy beaches, many are pebble beaches, but they all share the beautiful waters of the Aegean Sea.

– Corfu –

39.6239574, 19.9201090 / 39° 37' 26.247" N 19° 55' 12.392" E

Corfu is located off the northwestern coast of Greece and covers about 230 square miles. Evidence shows it has been inhabited since the Paleolithic Era. Later, it was an important trade center for the Phoenicians.

Corfu was established about 734 BC as a colony belonging to Corinth. During the Peloponnesian War, Corfu joined with Athens. From 1386 to 1797 Venetians ruled the island. In 1864, the island united with Greece.

Because of its being under the control of many governments over the centuries — including British, Russian-Ottoman, French, and Venetian — one can see these influences in the architecture, cuisine, and culture of Corfu.

The vibrant colors and majectic statues accent the beauty of Achilleion Palace.

— PHOTO BY KATARZYNATYL / PIXABAY

Archaeology in Corfu —

The city of Kassiopi is home to some of the most significant archaeological sites on Corfu. Temples, fortifications, and residential buildings from both Greek and Roman periods have been discovered.

During the Napoleonic Wars in the early 1800s, French soldiers were digging trenches for battle and discovered ruins from the Temple of Artemis. Beginning about 1910, excavation of the site took place under the direction of Greek archaeologist Federiko Versakis (Greek Archaeological Society) and German archaeologist Wilhelm Dörpfeld (German Archaeological Institute).

Because of its rich history, numerous sites and ruins have been identified over the past couple of centuries.

Sites to See —

Church of the Holy Apostles Jason and Sosipater —
39.6097116, 19.9244450 / 39° 36' 34.962" N 19° 55' 28.002" E

When Paul concluded his letter to the Christians at Rome, he sent greetings to a number of people. He then stated, "Timothy, my fellow worker, greets you; so do Lucius and Jason and Sosipater, my kinsmen" (Romans 16:21). This is the only time Sosipater is mentioned in the Bible, although some believe Sopater in Acts 20:4 is the same person. We read about Jason in Acts 17 when Paul was preaching in Thessalonica.

Around 1000, the Church of the Holy Apostles Jason and Sosipater was constructed to honor Jason and Sosipater. Tradition says they traveled to Corfu and established the church there about 63 AD.

There are a couple of references to *Acts of Jason and Sosipater*, an apocryphal text that was composed somewhere around the 4th or 5th century. I could not find where there are any copies of this work, but their story has been told throughout the generations. It is a story of fervent preaching, conversion of pagans, the challenge of imprisonment, being boiled in a cauldron of hot tar, the governor's daughter being killed by her own father because of her faith, the governor drowning at sea while pursuing other Christians… many factors.

Archaeological Museum of Corfu —
39.6188436, 19.9219145 / 39° 37' 7.837" N 19° 55' 18.892" E

Construction on the museum began in 1962 and was completed in 1965. The museum was originally designed to feature finds from the Temple of Artemis in Corfu. Among the items displayed are the Gorgon pediment from the Temple of Artemis at Corfu, the Lion of Menecrates, some terracotta statuettes of Artemis, and a collection of coins.

Achilleion Palace —

39.5627618, 19.9042738 / 39° 33′ 45.942″ N   19° 54′ 15.386″ E

In 1890, Empress Elisabeth of Austria built Achilleion Palace to use as a summer residence. With a combination of art nouveau and neo-classical styles, the palace is home to magnificent statues, beautiful paintings, lush floral gardens, and the Keiser Wilhelm II Museum. It is located in Gastouri, a few miles southwest of the town of Corfu.

Palaio Frourio / Old Fortress —

39.6234195, 19.9258931 / 39° 37′ 24.310″ N   19° 55′ 33.215″ E

This 14th century fortress is situated on a rocky outcropping in the City of Corfu just down from Spianada Square. The Old Fortress bridge carries you across the Contrafossa Moat, and you feel like you're going back in time — into the Middle Ages. There are indications of fortifications as early as the 6th century.

Hop On, Hop Off Bus —

There is a double-decker hop-on, hop-off bus that will take you around the city of Corfu to see the sites.

Beach / Water —

Corfu is surrounded by the beautiful Ionian Sea and has a number of beaches which you can enjoy. Go swimming, sailing, and paragliding.

— Crete —

35.3337415, 25.1432351 / 35° 20′ 1.469″ N   25° 8′ 35.646″ E

Crete is the 88th largest island in the world and the fifth largest in the Mediterranean Sea. It is the largest of the approximately 6,000 Greek islands and is around 160 miles long and 37 miles wide at its greatest width. It has a population of about 650,000.

Although there is evidence of settlements in Crete thousands of years ago, the first recorded civilization is that of the Minoans. This was about 3000 BC. Over the centuries, Crete was under the rule of different governments including Rome, the Byzantine Empire, and Ottoman Turks. In 1898, Crete became independent. However, because of its historic ties to the Greek culture, Crete chose to unite with Greece in 1913.

The Koules Fortress stands guard at the entrance to the harbor at Heraklion, Crete. This Venetian fortress was built in the 16th century.

— PHOTO BY KAY MILLS

Paul in Crete —

In our previous chapter, "Islands of Paul," we relate Paul's journey to Rome. It was on this trip that Paul — not as a missionary, but as a prisoner — stopped at Crete as the ship made its way along the southern coastline of Crete (Acts 27:7, 12, 13, 21). Even though Paul did not take this journey as a missionary, he was always a disciple of Jesus Christ faithfully proclaiming the word of God when doors opened.

The first Christians on Crete may have been converted on the Day of Pentecost as some were present for Peter's preaching (Acts 2:11). Although it is not recorded, Paul may have had the opportunity to visit with some of the Christians in one or more of their stops in Crete. Paul spoke about leaving Titus in Crete to help the churches and appoint elders in every city (Titus 1:5). Did Titus travel with Paul on this trip as far as Crete? We don't know.

Archaeology in Crete —

Because of its size, history, culture, sites to see, and the number of archaeological sites, Crete really deserves its own guide book. However, a large percentage of people will just be making a half-day or one-day stop on their cruise.

On Saturday, July 12, 2025, the UNESCO World Heritage Committee recognized these six major archaeological sites on Crete: Knossos, Phaistos, Malia, Zakros, Zominthos, and Kydonia, because of their value and being home to Minoan palace centers.

These and other sites, including Gortyn, Aptera, Palekastro, Eleutherna, and the Matala Caves, contribute to the understanding of history and culture on Crete throughout the centuries.

The earliest archaeological excavations on Crete took place in 1878-1879 at Knossos by Mínos Kalokerinós on a hill called Kephala tou Tselebi. Kalokerinós' family owned this piece of land. Kalokerinós had an interest in ancient Greek authors, and in *Kalokairinos 1893* he stated, "I undertook the excavation of Homer's great city of Knossos, the seat of King Minos." After about three weeks of excavations he discovered what turned out to be the west wing of a Minoan palace.

The area was under Ottoman rule, and under their pressure Kalokerinós stopped his work. Over the next couple of years Kalokerinós contacted scholars to let them know of his discoveries, but it would be years before further excavations were pursued.

In 1894, Sir Arthur Evans made his first trip to Crete. In 1899, he purchased the land where the palace was later found. In 1900, he and his team started digging and found the throne room of the palace. Their work continued from 1900 to 1913, and then again from 1922 to 1930.

This is a replica of the Phaistos Disc which was discovered by Luigi Pernier in 1908.

Other archaeologists have contributed to the discoveries on Crete.

Iosif Hatzidakis was digging for gold and discovered a Minoan palace at Malia. It is the third largest Minoan palace on Crete and dates to 1650-1450 BC. It had been built on top of an earlier palace. Hatzidakis also dug at other sites on Crete.

Stephanos Xanthoudides excavated at Koumasa from 1904 to 1906. From 1923 to 1925 he worked at Tylisos. He also worked with Hatzidakis in establishing the Heraklion Archaeological Museum.

On July 3, 1908, Luigi Pernier discovered the Phaistos Disc during excavations at Phaistos. The disc dates to 1850 BC to 1600 BC and is a little over six inches in diameter. The text/images flow in a spiral pattern on each side of the disc. Dr. Gareth Owens, who has studied the disc for about 30 years claimed in 2024 to have deciphered 99% of its content.

Nikolaos Platon was recognized for discovering the palace at Zakros.

Leyland Hugh Sackett excavated at the Minoan site of Palaikastro from 1962 to 1963 and from 1983 to 2020. A collection of his slides is housed at Rhodes College in Memphis, Tennessee.

Sites to See —

Knossos Palace —

35.2982550, 25.1614594 / 35° 17′ 53.718″ N 25° 9′ 41.254″ E

Visit the Palace of Knossos and peek into the ancient Minoan Civilization. This is one of the most important archaeological sites in Greece. Parts have been reconstructed to give one an image of its size and grandeur. There are many artifacts and areas of the palace to see as you make your way through this enormous maze. Sometimes this tour is combined with visits to **Heraklion** (35.3425332, 25.1446526 / 35° 20′ 33.120″ N 25° 8′ 40.749″ E) and the **Heraklion Archaeological Museum** (35.3387342, 25.1369489 / 35° 20′ 19.443″ N 25° 8′ 13.016″ E) which houses many items from the Minoan civilization.

Akrotiri Peninsula —

35.5254068, 24.0776643 / 35° 31′ 31.464″ N 24° 4′ 39.591″ E

This rocky peninsula is close to the port of Chania and has a lot to offer. Three monasteries — **Agias Triada** (35.5607445, 24.1347699 / 35° 33′ 38.680″ N 24° 8′ 5.172″ E), **Virgin of the Angels Monastery / Gouverneto** (35.5843475, 24.1401792 / 35° 35′ 3.651″ N 24° 8′ 24.645″ E), and **Katholika** (35.5901873, 24.1461129 / 35° 35′ 24.674″ N 24° 8′ 46.006″ E) — are located here.

On the hill Profiti Ilia (Prophet Elijah) on the western side of the peninsula is the tomb of **Elefthérios Venizélos** (35.5247712, 24.0560202 / 35° 31′ 29.176″ N 24° 3′ 21.673″ E) who served as Prime Minister of Greece for 12 years between 1910 and 1933. The Athens airport carries his name.

You can also dance on the sandy beach at **Stravos Bay** (35.5916591, 24.0952788 / 35° 35′ 29.973″ N 24° 5′ 43.004″ E) where Anthony Quinn danced in the 1964 movie *Zorba the Greek*.

Chinai Old Town —

Enjoy the history and culture of this area filled with beautifully restored buildings from the Venetian period. The 16th century **Firkas Fortress** (35.5189817, 24.0155036 / 35° 31′ 8.334″ N 24° 0′ 55.813″ E) is located opposite the Chania Lighthouse. The fortress offers great panoramic views of the area including the Old Town, Chania Lighthouse, and the ocean.

Rethymno & Ancient Eleutherna —

One of the most important archaeological sites in Crete is **Eleutherna** (35.3265324, 24.6762824 / 35° 19′ 35.517″ N 24° 40′ 34.617″ E). Ruins discovered include luxurious villas, baths, and other public buildings. Finds have given insight into burial customs during the Greek Dark Ages, about the 11th century BC to the 9th century BC. Although it is not officially opened to visitors, many do visit the site each year.

The grandeur of the Palace of Knossos is evident as you walk around the grounds. The top photo is of the throne room.

— PHOTOS BY KAY MILLS

Nearby is the **Eleutherna Archaeological Museum** (35.3241178, 24.6703382 / 35° 19′ 26.824″ N 24° 40′ 13.218″ E) which houses many finds from the area.

Church of Panagías Kerás —

35.1567519, 25.6551925 / 35° 9′ 24.307″ N 25° 39′ 18.693″ E

This Byzantine church is well-known for its frescoes illustrating biblical events. Among the frescoes are the baptism of Jesus, the raising of Lazarus, Jesus' entry into Jerusalem, the Crucifixion, Michael announcing the second coming, and a view of heaven picturing Abraham, Isaac, and Jacob.

Samaria Gorge Hike —

The Samaria Gorge is one of Europe's longest gorges and features beautiful rugged landscape in the White Mountains of Crete. This is a 10-mile hike, the path is clearly marked, there are rest stops along the way, and you finish on a beautiful beach. The main starting point is **Xyloskalo** (35.3079367, 23.9183719 / 35° 18′ 28.572″ N   23° 55′ 6.139″ E).

Food, Olive Oil, Architecture —

Whether your ship docks at Chania or Heraklion, you can find tours that feature the local cuisine, olive oil experiences, or history and architecture.

— Milos —

36.6940259, 24.4006051 / 36° 41′ 38.493″ N 24° 24′ 2.178″ E

Milos is a volcanic island that has been inhabited since the Neolithic period. It was an ancient source for obsidian which is a volcanic glass. This made Milos a trade center in the early days.

During the Peloponnesian War, Milos aligned with Athens. Later, under Roman rule, Milos thrived economically because of its mining bentonite and perlite. During the Byzantine period the island was challenged by marauding pirates. It later was under Venetian control before being under Ottoman control. During the Greek War of Independence, Milos joined Greece.

Milos offers a lot of water activities around the island. This photo gives a glimpse into the beauty of the area.

— PHOTO BY MONIEK58 / PIXABAY

Archaeology in Milos —

On April 8, 1820, Yorgos Ketrotas, a Greek farmer, was digging in his field and found what is perhaps the most important discovery on Milos: the Venus de Milo. This exquisite example of Hellenistic sculpture is now in the Louvre in Paris.

Various organizations, including the British School at Athens and the French School at Athens, carried out archaeological excavations. Early Christian Roman-Era catacombs, carved into the volcanic rock, are unique in Greece.

From 1896 to 1899, the northern city of Phylakopi was excavated. It was a Bronze Age settlement, and artifacts included beautiful pottery. This excavation is of note, not just because of what was discovered, but because of how archaeologist Duncan MacKenzie recorded detailed stratigraphic information.

Excavations are continuing on Milos under the auspices of the Ephorate of Antiquities of Cyclades.

Sites to See —

Cultural and Archaeology Tour —

Take a tour in which you visit several sites on Milos: **Plaka Castle** (36.7457093, 24.4227842 / 36° 44′ 44.553″ N   24° 25′ 22.023″ E) overlooks the village of Plaka. The castle is built on the second highest hill on Milos and offers breathtaking views. The **Milos Catacombs** (36.7373164, 24.4237516 / 36° 44′ 14.339″N 24° 25′ 25.506″E) were discovered in 1844 and are about 2,000 years old. They are a testament to the Christian history of the islands and served as a burial site for early Christians. Tickets are about €10 for a brief but informative tour. Just a short distance from the catacombs is the **Ancient Theatre of Milos** (36.7377648, 24.4210115 / 36° 44′ 15.953″N 24° 25′ 15.641″E). Originally built in the 3rd century BC, this white marble theatre was discovered in 1814. It currently seats about 700 and periodically hosts cultural events. Between the theatre and the parking lot is where the **Venus de Milo** was found (36.7387023, 24.4224457 / 36° 44′ 19.328″N 24° 25′ 20.805″E).

North Shore Tour —

This tour takes you along the north shore of Milos. **Phylakopi** (36.7568843, 24.5105203 / 36° 45′ 24.783″ N   24° 30′ 37.873″ E) is where Lady of Phylakopi was discovered. She is a terracotta statue about 5-1/2 inches tall and is now in the Archaeological Museum of Milos. **Papafragas Caves** (36.7540108, 24.5034663 / 36° 45′ 14.439″ N   24° 30′ 12.479″ E) were shaped by volcanic activity and is an area of sea caves. **Sarakiniko Beach** (36.7426735, 24.4584189 / 36° 44′ 33.625″ N   24° 27′ 30.308″ E) is an area with a unique geological structure of pure white rock formations. **Mandrakia** (36.7508321, 24.4461620 / 36° 45′ 2.996″ N   24° 26′

46.183″E) is a colorful little fishing village. While there, you may want to try some seafood.

Cruising Milos —

Enjoy the beautiful blue Aegean Sea aboard a catamaran. You can swim, snorkel, and paddle board while on this cruise.

— Mykonos —

37.4513494, 25.3276080 / 37° 27' 4.858" N   25° 19' 39.389" E

Mykonos has a history of nearly 6,000 years. During Roman and Byzantine rule, Mykonos and neighboring Delos played a major role in being a trade hub. In the 13th century the island was under Venetian control and then under Ottoman rule in the 16th century.

Mykonos is famous for its 16th century whitewashed windmills.

The Greek War of Independence brought about a change to the ruling government. Manto Mavrogenous was an aristocrat who used her finances to help fund the war.

Agriculture and fishing have played an economic role in Mykonos.

During the 1950s and 1960s, tourism began to boom in Mykonos as it became the hot spot for Europeans to vacation.

Archaeology in Mykonos —

Although it is not on Mykonos, the small island of Delos is a dedicated archaeological site and a UNESCO World Heritage Site.

The excavations on Delos started in 1873 by the French School of Archaeology. The most important monuments of the site are the Agora, the Temple of Apollo, the Terrace of the Lions and the ancient theatre, which is being renovated currently to host theatre performances. On Delos, there is a small museum with findings from the island.

Sites to see —

Old Town Strolling —

Get off the boat, and go to the old town by the harbor. Enjoy the 16th century windmills, take in the view, stop in a shop or two, sit down at one of the cafes for coffee or a meal…

My wife and I enjoy strolling around the harbor area with the whitewashed buildings, various shops and cafes, and its little Greek Orthodox church building on the waterfront.

— PHOTO BY DALE W. MANOR

Museum Tour —

Spend time at the **Mykonos Agricultural Museum** (37.4465968, 25.3308080 / 37° 26′ 47.748″ N   25° 19′ 50.909″ E) which has both inside and outside displays of agricultural equipment. The **Aegean Maritime Museum** (37.4452603, 25.3283831 / 37° 26′ 42.937″ N   25° 19′ 42.179″ E) was established by Mykonian George M. Dracopoulos and his spouse Ioanna. It features the restored Armenistis Lighthouse which was built in 1890. Exhibits include models of ships from the early Minoan period until the beginning of the 20th century. Navigation instruments, charts, and historic documents are on display.

The **Folklore Museum** (37.4473922, 25.3257968 / 37° 26′ 50.612″ N 25° 19′ 32.868″ E) is housed in the home of an 18th century seafaring captain. Many contents are from the 19th century. Items include historical photographs, traditional musical instruments, vintage furniture, antique tools, embroidered work, and ceramics. There are also many pieces of maritime equipment. **The Archaeological Museum of Mykonos** (37.4499326, 25.3294211 / 37° 26′ 59.757″ N 25° 19′ 45.916″ E) was built in 1902. One prominent display is a large vase produced on the neighboring island of Tinos which pictures scenes of the fall of Troy. The museum contains a number of artifacts including some from the neighboring island of Rhenia.

Delos Archaeology Tour —

37.3988367, 25.2651513 / 37° 23′ 55.812″ N 25° 15′ 54.545″ E

Located just a few miles from Mykonos, Delos is — according to Greek mythology — the birthplace of Apollo, the god of light. Tours to Delos are typically a round trip from Mykonos Old Port.

This small island is an important archaeological site. While there you can stroll through the narrow streets of the city to the market place. You will see the house of Dionysos, a statue of Cleopatra, beautiful mosaics, and the Stoa of Phillipe. The Temple of Apollo and the Naxian Lions are impressive.

Take time to visit the archaeological museum and maybe pick up a couple items in the museum shop before boarding your boat to return to Mykonos.

– Patmos –

37.3233625, 26.5438619 / 37° 19′ 24.105″ N   26° 32′ 37.903″ E

Patmos is a part of the Dodecanese island group and one of its smaller islands. Because of its irregular shape, it has 163 miles of coastline with numerous beaches for swimming, diving, and snorkeling.

Greek mythology says the island was once submerged, but Artemis, the goddess of the hunt, brought it up out of the sea. It shows evidence of being inhabited during the Mycenaean period.

As you're making your way to the Cave of the Apocalypse,
you get an excellent view of the beautiful harbor in Patmos.

The Apostle John in Patmos —

Most of us would never have heard of Patmos had the apostle John not been exiled there by the Roman Emperor Domitian. The Revelation of Jesus Christ would have been written anyway — whether from Patmos, Ephesus, or some other place. It was a message for the church at that time, and it is a message from which we can learn today.

John addressed this treatise to the seven churches in Asia: Ephesus, Smyrna, Pergamum, Thyatira, Sardis, Philadelphia, and Laodicea (Revelation 1:11).

The gospel writers record the life and ministry of Jesus Christ. Many times our minds generate an image of Jesus based on where He is and what He is doing. I'm guessing none of our images compare to the one John paints in these few words: "Then I turned to see the voice that was speaking to me, and on turning I saw seven golden lampstands, and in the midst of the lampstands one like a son of man, clothed with a long robe and with a golden sash around his chest. The hairs of his head were white, like white wool, like snow. His eyes were like a flame of fire, his feet were like burnished bronze, refined in a furnace, and his voice was like the roar of many waters. In his right hand he held seven stars, from his mouth came a sharp two-edged sword, and his face was like the sun shining in full strength" (Revelation 1:12-16).

When you enter the Cave of the Apocalypse, be sure an take a look at the beautiful mosaic over the doorway.

Sites to See —

Following are some sites you can see on your own or on an organized tour:

Skala —

37.3233729, 26.5449287 / 37° 19′ 24.142″ N 26° 32′ 41.743″ E

Skala is the primary harbor on Patmos and also its business center. As you arrive here, you'll notice the whitewashed buildings, small cafes, various little shops, and winding streets.

Cave of the Apocalypse —
37.3144464, 26.5447053 / 37° 18′ 52.007″ N   26° 32′ 40.939″ E

The Cave of the Apocalypse is probably the main tourist site on Patmos.. Tradition says this is where John the Apostle wrote The Revelation after being exiled by Domitian. It is a small cave filled with icons. A lot of what you hear during the tour will be tradition.

Your guide may point out the cracks in the ceiling and note that it cracked when Jesus gave John The Revelation. Perhaps they will show you the stone slab that was to have been John's bed and the silver framed handhold by which he pulled himself up. Whatever took place in that cave — or elsewhere on the island — we know that John was a faithful servant who diligently recorded the words of The Revelation near the end of his life.

Chora —
37.3092922, 26.5478338 / 37° 18′ 33.452″ N   26° 32′ 52.202″ E

North of Skala, and with the Cave of the Apocalypse half way between, is the capital city of Chora. It is here where you will find the Holy Monastery of Saint John the Theologian. This medieval structure was built in 1088 by Hosios Christodoulos Latrinos. It is a place of study and pilgrimage for Greek Orthodox. Three windmills stand on top of a hill east of the monastery. The oldest two date back to 1688.

— Rhodes —
36.4316495, 28.2158117 / 36° 25′ 53.938″ N 28° 12′ 56.922″ E

Rhodes is the fourth largest Greek island and the largest of the Do-decanese islands. It was home to the Colossus of Rhodes, one of the Seven Wonders of the World. This 105-foot-tall bronze statue was completed in 280 BC and stood at the entrance of Mandraki Harbor at Rhodes. It commemorated the successful defense of the city which had been besieged for about a year by Demetrius I of Macedon.

Rhodes — as do many of the islands — shows evidence of habitation during the Neolithic period. During the Bronze Age, Rhodes gained prominence when it became part of the Minoan civilization. Lindos, Ialysos, and Kamiros were city-states that were established on the island by the 8th century BC. During the Hellenistic period, Rhodes had a navy and well-recognized schools of rhetoric and philosophy. It was during this time that the Colossus of Rhodes was constructed.

In 1310, Rhodes, along with some neighboring islands, was con-quered by The Order of the Knights of the Hospital of Saint John of Jerusalem, better known as the Knights Hospitaller. In 1522, Sulei-man the Magnificent conquered the island. It was controlled by the Ottomans for almost four centuries.

After periods of control by Italy and the British, Rhodes became part of Greece in 1947. It is a UNESCO World Heritage Site.

Apollonius of Rhodes is best known for his epic poem, Argonautica. This poem is about Jason and the Argonauts who, on an order of King Pelias, set off on a quest to find the Golden Fleece.

Paul in Rhodes —

After the apostle Paul completed his visit with the elders of Ephesus at Miletus and the emotional farewell, we are told the next stop in his journey to Jerusalem: "And when we had parted from them and set sail, we came by a straight course to Cos, and the next day to Rhodes, and from there to Patara" (Acts 21:1). Tradition has Paul and his companions landing in a small, sheltered bay at Lindos, Rhodes — about 25 miles from Mandraki Harbor. This is the only reference to Rhodes in the Bible, and as was Luke's custom, he noted even the overnight anchorages of the ship.

Archaeology in Rhodes —

Some of the earliest archaeological work on Rhodes took place at Ancient Kamiros. The initial discovery was made by British archaeologists Alfred Biliotti and Augustus Salzmann in the 1850s. Italian archaeologist Luigi Morricone conducted excavations from 1928-1934. Kamiros was a Hellenistic city which showed advanced urban planning.

The Lindos Acropolis and Temple of Athena Lindia were excavated from 1900-1905 by Karl Frederik Kinch who received his education at the University of Copenhagen. This area was a major religious and cultural center.

Other excavations took place at Ancient Ialyssos which was one of the three earliest city-states on Rhodes. It was located on Mount Filerimos.

Perhaps some of the most intriguing excavations were the Medieval City and Palace of the Grand Master in Rhodes Old Town. It is a rather well preserved Crusader city. Initial excavations took place in the 1930s by Italian archaeologists Giorgio Rizzardi and Armando Bernabiti among others.

Sites to See —

Tour the Harbor Area —

As cruise ships dock at Rhodes, they dock just a little distance from where the Colossus of Rhodes, one of the Seven Wonders of the World, once stood. To the northwest of the cruise ship dock is the Rhodes Marina.

There are three opinions as to where the Colossus of Rhodes stood:

◆ At the entrance to Mandraki Harbour there are two Rhodian Deer Statues, and some believe this is where the Colossus was located. The left foot would have been at the **Stag Statue** site

(36.4510426, 28.2258656 / 36° 27′ 3.753″ N   28° 13′ 33.116″ E), and the right foot would have been at the **Doe Statue** site (36.4511597, 28.2265422 / 36° 27′ 4.175″ N   28″ 13′ 35.552″ E). Some object to this being the site because of the difficulty of keeping the harbor open during construction of the statue.

◆ Others believe the Colossus stood where **Saint Nicholas Fortress** is located (36.4511557, 28.2278835 / 36° 27′ 4.161″ N   28° 13′ 40.381″ E). This fortress was constructed in the 1460s by Grand Master of the Order of St. John Zacosta. The lighthouse at the fortress began operating in 1675 and has been rebuilt in the last several years.

◆ A few believe that the Colossus stood on the Acropolis of Rhodes overlooking the city and harbor.

The Rhodes Windmills (36.4491781, 28.2279395 / 36.4491781,28.2279395) are to the south of Saint Nicholas Fortress. Originally built to grind corn for export, they are now majestic reminders of time gone by. You can sit on area benches and enjoy the harbor.

Medieval City Tour —

This great city opens the door to the days of knights in shining armor. The **Sea Gate** (36.4440309, 28.2282994 / 36° 26′ 38.511″ N   28° 13′ 41.878″ E) is one of four gates through which you can enter the city.

The Archaeological Museum of Rhodes (36.4447880, 28.2272305 / 36° 26′ 41.237″ N   28° 13′ 38.030″ E) is just a little northwest of the Sea Gate entrance. It has artifacts, mosaics, and rooms full of statues.

You are truly transported back to a different time as you walk on the **Street of the Knights of Rhodes** (36.4450519, 28.2270152 / 36° 26′ 42.187″ N   28° 13′ 37.255″ E). Every stone has a story. After walking west for a few hundred feet, you come to the **Palace of the Grand Master of the Knights of Rhodes** (36.4457027, 28.2239760 / 36° 26′ 44.530″ N   28° 13′ 26.314″ E). It is an imposing site on the outside but not a lot to see on the inside.

Inside the Old Town is also the **Square of the Hebrew Martyrs** (36.4455045, 28.2270688 / 36° 26′ 43.816″ N   28° 13′ 37.448″ E). This is in memory of the many Jews who were transported from Rhodes to Nazi concentration camps during World War II. Nearby is the **Temple of Aphrodite** (36.4459114, 28.2273634 / 35° 26′ 45.281″ N   28° 13′ 38.508″ E). This ancient temple gives you a sense of another time in history.

Outside the walls is the **De Naillac Tower** (36.4463507, 28.2292301 / 36° 26′ 46.863″ N 28° 13′ 45.228″ E). This is a great tower to climb for fantastic photos. Watch your step!

This small cove is St Paul's Bay, and it is believed this is where the ship docked for the night as they sailed to Jerusalem (Acts 21:1).   — PHOTO BY DALE W. MANOR

St Paul Tour in Lindos —

From a biblical history perspective, **St Paul's Bay at Lindos** (36.0871350, 28.0879273 / 36° 5′ 13.686″ N 28° 5′ 16.538″ E) is the main site to see here. the bay is considered to be the site where Paul and his companions stopped for the night when returning to Jerusalem. Overlooking the bay is **Chapel of Agios Pavlos** (36.0861995, 28.0888429 / 36° 5′ 10.318″ N 28° 5′ 19.834″ E).

The **Ancient Theatre of Lindos** (36.0897936, 28.0871248 / 36° 5′ 23.257″ N 28° 5′ 13.649″ E) dates back to the 4th century BC. Just northeast of the theatre is the **Acropolis of Lindos** (36.0915070, 28.0885342 / 36° 5′ 29.425″ N 28° 5′ 18.723″ E). Various ruins are on the Acropolis including a Roman temple and the **Temple of Athena Lindia** (36.0911572, 28.0881989 / 36° 5′ 28.166″ N 28° 5′ 17.516″ E).

North of the Acropolis is Pallas Beach and **Sea Caves** (36.0947175, 28.0907732 / 36° 5′ 40.983″ N 28° 5′ 26.784″ E). This offers a great swimming and snorkeling area.

— Santorini —

36.4158203, 25.4319138 / 36° 24′ 56.953″ N   25° 25′ 54.890″ E

With an area of about 28 square miles, Santorini has a population of a little over 15,000 people. The island's official name is Thira (or Thera). Before the volcanic explosion that took place around 1600 BC, the island was known as Strogili, which means "round" or "circular." During Ottoman times, it was also known as Dermetzik.

While at Oia, you can take a look across the caldera to get an idea of how powerful the volcanic eruption was that created this beautiful landscape.

The shape of Santorini is the result of a volcanic eruption that took place about 1600 BC. Scientists continue to monitor the volcano but are more concerned about the possibility of a major earthquake. Santorini is within a seismic zone known as the Hellenic Volcanic Arc, and hundreds of undersea earthquakes have been recorded in the area in 2025.

Santorini reflects the cultures of Phoenicians, Dorians, Romans, and Byzantines because of these civilizations having settled on the island throughout its history.

Archaeology on Santorini —

The 1600 BC eruption covered the Minoan city of Akrotiri in ash and created what has been called "The Greek Pompeii" by some. It has become the island's most important archaeological site.

Early archaeological excavations in Akrotiri were undertaken in 1867 by French geologist and petrologist Ferdinand André Fouqué. He discovered a rather well-preserved city. Spyridon Marinatos pursued this excavation from 1967 to 1974. Further excavations have taken place throughout the years, and many items are now in the Museum of Prehistoric Thera in the capital city of Fira. Some wall paintings are displayed in the National Archaeological Museum in Athens.

Getting a photo of the three blue-domed church buildings is on the bucket list for a lot of people.

A lot of things define Santorini: the three blue-domed church buildings at Oia, cliffside villages, vineyards where the grapes grow in a "kouloura" — a type of nest that protects them from the wind and sun, and some of the most stunning sunsets in the world.

Sites to See —

Touring Oia —

36.4636719, 25.3761239 / 36° 27′ 49.219″ N 25° 22′ 34.046″ E

A tour of Oia may be the number one destination of most tourists coming off of ships. Your bus will take you to the city where you can stroll the streets, get a cup of gelato, mingle with the crowd in the plaza in front of The Virgin Mary of the Akathist Hymn Church, get a great view of the caldera, and snap a photo of the three blue-domed church buildings.

Sailing the Caldera —

Board a catamaran, and enjoy scenic views and fresh sea breezes while sailing around the caldera. Take a dip in the private bay of Saint Nikolas. Savor great food while on the catamaran.

Exploring Akrotiri Ruins —

36.3518982, 25.4029939 / 36° 21′ 6.834″ N 25° 24′ 10.778″ E

Visit this Bronze Age settlement that was destroyed by — yet preserved by a volcanic eruption. Take a guided tour along Akrotiri's cobblestone streets, see the frescoes, peek into ancient shops.

Highlights of Santorini —

From Akrotini to Oia to Fira, see the highlights of this glorious island, enjoy breathtaking views, stroll the streets, celebrate wonderful Greek food...

So many more...

With around 6,000 islands, there are so many one can visit for the culture, food, history... for sailing, swimming, beaches... for walking, hiking, rock climbing... Greece is a wonderful place to tour.

We could fill many books on beautiful islands such as Lipsi, Paxos, Thassos, Naxos, Zakynthos, Karpathos, Skiathos, Ikaria, Paros, Sifnos, Kefalonia, Lefkada, Alonnisos, Kastellorizo, Chalki... Maybe... one day.

But today... enjoy, be blessed, and be a blessing.

Chapter 31

Paul's Unknown Churches

Paul and his missionary journeys are well known. Many of us, when we were in elementary school, memorized these journeys, facts about what took place in various cities, and lessons to be learned from Paul's ministry.

But are there other churches about which we know nothing — or very little?

Nicopolis —

After being released from his first Roman imprisonment, Paul wrote Titus stating he was planning on spending the winter in Nicopolis. This is on the western coast of Greece, a few miles north of the modern city of Preveza. He asked Titus to come see him (Titus 3:12).

We don't read about Paul's making tents in Nicopolis. We don't read about Paul's teaching in Nicopolis. We don't read about Paul's developing friendships and relationships in Nicopolis.

But Paul cherished his salvation and was an evangelist at heart. If Paul spent a day in Nicopolis, he spoke the saving message of Jesus Christ to someone. If Paul spent a week there, he probably found a public gathering where he could speak. If he spent the winter there, he undoubtedly preached the word, taught many people, and most assuredly established a church there.

Crete —

As focused as Paul was on proclaiming the gospel of Jesus Christ, he became a lightening rod for criticism and condemnation by those opposed to Jesus. He was arrested, and in Acts 25:11, he appealed to Caesar.

As the prisoners were being transported to Rome, the ship apparently made at least one stop in Crete (Acts 27:7-21). This is the only reference we have of Paul's possibly being in Crete.

Later in life, he wrote Titus stating, "This is why I left you in Crete, so that you might put what remained into order, and appoint elders in every town as I directed you" (Titus 1:5). At some point a church was established in Crete, and Paul was instrumental in its establishment.

Illyricum —

During Paul's life, Illyricum was a Roman province located northwest of any of Paul's recorded travels. When writing the Christians in Rome, Paul testified, "so that from Jerusalem and all the way around to Illyricum I have fulfilled the ministry of the gospel of Christ" (Romans 15:19).

Does this mean that he went into Illyricum or that his preaching approached its borders or that some of his coworkers evangelized in Illyricum? We don't know. However, the probability is that as he traveled through Macedonia, he was proclaiming the message in a region that bordered Illyricum.

When John closed his gospel of Jesus Christ, he concluded, "Now there are also many other things that Jesus did. Were every one of them to be written, I suppose that the world itself could not contain the books that would be written" (John 21:25).

Could the same be said of the apostle Paul?

Chapter 32

Paul's Faithful Coworkers

If people were asked what one or two words define the apostle Paul's life and ministry, some of characteristics that might be mentioned would be dedicated, determined, committed, passionate, patient, courageous…

One attribute that stands out is his being a "people person." This shows up more so later in his ministry than in the earlier days.

Because Paul was a leader, he may have been more of a delegator or manager in his earlier days. However, as he grew in ministry and service, you see his working alongside others as he served in the kingdom.

When he wrote the Christians at Philippi, he appealed to the "true yokefellow" (KJV, ASV, and others) — σύζυγος — also translated companion or partner in some translations. This is the only time this Greek word is used in the New Testament, and it is a word which defines the closest of relationships.

When Paul wrote the Christians at Rome, he concluded the letter by commending Phoebe and sending greetings to Priscilla and Aquila who were coworkers. He continued to list a couple of dozen people and groups who held a special place in his heart.

In looking at his life, there is a major question that comes up: What type of Christian, what type of apostle, what type of evangelist would Paul have been without Barnabas? It was Barnabas who went and brought Paul back after he had been rejected. It was Barnabas who introduced him to other Christians. It was Barnabas whom the Holy Spirit set alongside Paul for mission work. It was Barnabas who mentored Paul. Barnabas' real name was Joseph, but the apostles gave him the name Barnabas which meant "son of encouragement" because that was his personality.

Paul and Barnabas had a rough streak because of John Mark's leaving them during the first missionary journey. After deciding they wanted to revisit the churches on a second journey, they went separate ways because Barnabas wanted to take John Mark, and Paul wasn't going to have any part of it.

Barnabas and John Mark headed to Cyprus. Paul and Silas departed through Syria and Cilicia on what is known as Paul's second missionary journey.

However, a seed had been planted in Paul's life. Paul became a strong encourager, hurts were healed, and Paul and John Mark reconciled. Toward the end of his life Paul wrote his faithful coworker Timothy and said, "Get Mark and bring him with you, for he is very useful to me for ministry" (2 Timothy 4:11).

In reviewing his ministry, Paul's coworkers served in many ways just as the body has many parts. Some traveled with him as evangelists; some provided lodging; some refreshed him; some encouraged him. These include:

◆ Barnabas, his coworker on the first missionary journey (Acts 13), his encourager, and his mentor

◆ John Mark, a coworker on the first journey — or at least part of it — who became a valuable partner years later

◆ Silas, also known as Silvanus, his partner on his second journey (Acts 15:40)

◆ Timothy, who joined him on his second journey (Acts 16:3) and worked with him throughout his life

◆ Aquila and Priscilla whom he met in Corinth (Acts 18:2)

◆ Titus, his "true child in a common faith" (Titus 1:4)

◆ Archippus, a fellow soldier (Philemon 2)

◆ Aristarchus, a companion and fellow prisoner (Colossians 4:10)

◆ Sopater the Berean; Aristarchus and Secundus of Thessalonica; Gaius of Derbe; and Tychicus and Trophimus of Asia — all who traveled with Paul as he was returning to Jerusalem (Acts 20:4)

◆ Euodia and Syntyche, who labored by his side (Philippians 4:2-3)

- Erastus, the city treasurer of Corinth whom Paul sent to Macedonia (Acts 19:22)

- Epaphras, a "beloved fellow servant" who probably established the church in Colossae (Colossians 1:7)

- Stephanas, Fortunatus, and Achaicus, because they refreshed his spirit (1 Corinthians 16:17-18)

- Luke, the beloved physician (Colossians 4:14) who accompanied Paul on some of his journeys

- Sosthenes, the ruler of the synagogue in Corinth (Acts 18:17) and one who was by Paul's side when he wrote 1 Corinthians (1 Corinthians 1:1)

- Epaphroditus, brother, fellow worker, fellow soldier, messenger, minister (Philippians 2:25)

- Mnason of Cyprus, who provided lodging to Paul (Acts 21:16)

- Apollos, a fellow evangelist referenced several times by Paul, perhaps the best known reference being 1 Corinthians 3:6

- Onesiphorus, who "often refreshed me and was not ashamed of my chains" (2 Timothy 1:16)

- Onesimus, a runaway slave who was useful to Paul (Philemon 11)

- Rufus and his mother, "who has been a mother to me as well" (Romans 16:13)

Time fails … perhaps a legion of other names could be added to this list, but as we look at the missionary journeys of Paul, the letters he wrote, and the focus on his life in the New Testament, we realize that there were many who supported, encouraged, and worked alongside him. He was who he was because of the power of the Holy Spirit and those who were his "true yokefellow."

Chapter 33

The End – And The Beginning

How far do we want to walk with Paul? In what situations do we want to walk with him? What life-changing events are we willing to face that Paul faced?

As we journey through Greece — or as we study his journeys as we study the Bible — may our eyes be opened not just to the sites he saw and the places he went — may our eyes be opened to our Lord and Savior Jesus Christ and His calling us to be His ambassadors every day in life wherever we are.

- ◆ Paul let Jesus work through him and many people were saved by the blood of Jesus Christ (Acts 21:19-20).

- ◆ Just as Paul encouraged the Christians at Corinth to be imitators of him as he was of Christ (1 Corinthians 11:1), so that same call comes to us almost 2,000 years later.

Whether or not you get to go to Greece and visit these places, may you always honor our Lord and Savior Jesus Christ in your life. May every day be a new beginning in Jesus and for Jesus.

And I am sure of this, that he who began a good work in you will bring it to completion at the day of Jesus Christ.

— PHILIPPIANS 1:6 —

Appendix

Travel Tips – Some Useful Hints

Following are some useful tips that we use and tips that will help you on any tour. This is not an exclusive list, and there are a number of other things that one may want to add. Also, there are other tips that would be country specific or activity specific. We want you to have the best tour possible.

Physical Condition —

You will enjoy the tour to the degree of the shape you're in. One scale I've used is the following:

◆ Maybe OK Shape — Able to walk a steady mile.
  NOTE: On some tours, because of cobblestone streets, gravel paths, hills, and steps, you would not be comfortable if this is all you can do. Also, keep in mind that on many tours, we are walking several miles a day when you total up your steps. (You will normally get your 10,000 steps!)

◆ OK Shape — Able to walk a steady mile up and down hills (including stairs).

◆ Better Shape — Able to walk two to four miles up and down hills (and stairs) that have cobblestones and marble sections.

◆ Best Shape — Able to run a marathon up Mount Olympus — or whatever mountain — and not be winded!

On most tours, you typically don't walk a long distance without stopping to visit a site, view an object, or talk about things.

Shoes —

You will want two (2) good pair of walking shoes. Break them in before the trip so you know they will be comfortable, but don't wear them out!

Walking Surfaces —

On many tours we will be walking up and down hills and over cobblestone streets. Also, as many of the streets, walkways, and sites are stone and marble, there will be places that are rather slick, so we need to take great care as we visit various sites.

Perfumes, Colognes, Sprays, and Oils —

Because some on our trip will be allergic to smells, odors, etc. and we will be next to each other and on a bus a lot of the time, we request that you not use perfume, after shave, body sprays, fragrant lotions, etc. on the trip. And this can even apply to essential oils. What may seem like a very faint or pleasant smell to you may be overpowering to someone else — sometimes creating an allergic reaction.

Travel Insurance —

We very strongly recommend the purchase of travel insurance for medical, emergency medical, trip delay, lost luggage, etc. I've used insurance twice: once because of a trip delay and last year because of medical issues. This insurance is not cheap, but I'd rather pay $1,000 (or whatever) for medical insurance than pay the $14,000 hospital/surgical bill.

Medical Transportation —

Your travel insurance probably pays for medical transportation that will transport you to the nearest hospital that can treat your needs. There are companies, like Medjet, that will do a hospital-to-hospital transfer to get you to your preferred facility.

Passport —

This is a good time to remind you that you will need a passport for any overseas travels, and the expiration date (in most situations) must be at least six (6) months after you return from your tour.

Visas —

The country to which your are going may require a Visa. Be sure and check on this.

TSA PreCheck® and Global Entry —

Many travelers use TSA PreCheck® or Global Entry. These give you a "Known Traveler Number." These programs are for U.S. citizens and U.S. lawful permanent residents. TSA PreCheck® gives you expedited security screening at more than 200 airports within the United States. Global Entry includes TSA PreCheck® and members can use Global Entry Customs Kiosks at more than 75 airports when returning to the U.S. from travel abroad.

How to Dress —

Business casual, khakis, nice jeans/pants — nothing with holes or overly worn. Men are to wear shirts with collars and sleeves. Ladies are to have blouses/tops with sleeves — nothing low cut. Bermuda shorts can be worn on some days in some situations. Many sites will require that both shoulders and knees be covered (men and women) and women may be required to wear a skirt at some sites. In this situation it would be good to carry a wrap-around skirt you can throw on. (Some sites have skirts they will give you to use.)

Words, Images, Messages on Clothing —

This includes shirts, jackets, pants, caps, etc. — Basically, no messages/images of any type. If you have a sweatshirt that has a state or school name ("Arkansas" or "Harding") that will be OK. And you may have a jacket with a company name on it. However, it is best not to have any mascots or artwork on any clothing. There should be no political messages of any type.

Rain Gear / Cool Weather Wear —

On some of our tours we will run into light showers or rain sometimes. I carry a very light plastic poncho I can throw over me. (It fits in a 4"x6" pouch.) As far as cooler weather goes, think layers.

Security —

There will be times when we will be in areas where pickpockets operate. The number one item you want to protect is your passport! Clothing Arts (clothingarts.com) has "pickpocket-proof pants." I wear 5.11 pants, and they work well for me. We can loan you money or clothing, but we can't loan you our passport! I make a photocopy of my Passport, Driver's License, and Insurance Cards and have a copy of that in each piece of luggage I carry, in my backpack, and on my phone.

Luggage —

How much luggage should you take on the trip? Some folks like to take anything they think they might need. Others can pack everything they want for a 2-week trip in a carry-on! Keep in mind, that you will be toting your luggage at times — sometimes for several blocks or up and down stairs.

We will provide you luggage tags, but you may do something else to identify your luggage, like paint a bright sunflower on it! On my luggage tag, I don't put my home address and phone number (I don't want people to have it) — I put the address and phone number of my home church. (I don't put the church name on the tag.)

Eating Overseas —

We've always had great food on the tours. However, to make sure my system can handle any changes, about a month before I leave, I begin taking probiotics to help build up good bacteria in my gut. This is not as critical in nations where the food is like or similar to what we are used to. However, we do this as a precaution even in places like Israel, England, or Greece.

Drinking Water —

We are able to drink the water in most hotels where we travel. When in doubt, drink bottled water. On the Nile cruise, don't even brush your teeth with the ship's water. Always stay hydrated.

Prescriptions —

TSA does not require prescriptions to be in prescription bottles. HOWEVER, laws of different states and different nations vary. So, please have all prescriptions in a prescription bottle for that medication. If your bottle is large (3 months supply / 3 times a day / horse tablet size), you may want to contact your pharmacist and get a smaller bottle with your prescription label on it and just carry a two-week — or however long — supply.

NOTE: Before your flight, verify anything that has to do with TSA, airline regulations, or laws in the countries you are visiting.

Traveling with Vitamins —

In order to save space, we put our vitamins in individual plastic bags with a label on each bag identifying the specific vitamin.

Sharp Objects and Other Prohibited Items —

Please familiarize yourself with items you can and cannot take on board the aircraft. You may normally carry a pocketknife with you.

Don't bring it. Don't check it. Even though you can check it, you may not be able to carry it in the country in which we are visiting. The TSA site will be a good resource on what you can/cannot carry.

Being Nice to Airline, Customs, and TSA Personnel —

I've found that being nice to these folks really makes traveling a lot more enjoyable. They have a job to do, and I try and help them do their job efficiently. And they have been very nice to me.

— Your Passport, again —

Don't forget your passport. If you do, Delta, United, American, Lufthansa, or whoever won't wait on you; the bus won't wait on you; we won't wait on you. (We love you, but we still won't wait on you!) Remember your passport!

Your Driver's License —

Just a quick reminder that you now need a REAL ID driver's license for airline flights. Your passport will substitute for this.

Start a "Go Box" —

About a month before you leave, set a box on a table or designate a specific spot for items to take on your trip. This will give you a place to put things when you suddenly remember you want to take _____ on the trip. Put a legal pad and a pen or pencil in your "Go Box" so you can jot down things when you remember them if they are not handy to drop in the box at that time.

Spending Money —

On most tours you can spend a lot of money on a variety of things. You will probably want about $15-$25 each day for meals/snacks. In some countries you can use US Dollars; in other countries, you will need to exchange your money for local currency. You will want money for souvenirs. You can find souvenirs for a few dollars up to several thousand dollars. Know your budget!

Your Phone —

Check with your phone provider so you will know what overseas services are available. You may prefer to buy a SIM card in the country to which you are going.

Notes —

Notes –

www.ingramcontent.com/pod-product-compliance
Lightning Source LLC
Chambersburg PA
CBHW070607130626
46556CB00001B/299